Cocktails, Cocktails & more Cocktails

An Imagine Book
Published by Charlesbridge
85 Main Street, Watertown, MA 02472
617-926-0329
www.charlesbridge.com

Created by Penn Publishing Ltd.
1 Yehuda Halevi Street, Tel Aviv, Israel 65135
www.penn.co.il

Design and layout by Michal & Dekel
Edited by Rachel Penn
Photography by Danya Weiner
Food styling by Deanna Linder

Library of Congress Cataloging-in-Publication Data Available

ISBN 978-1-62354-030-2 (Special Edition for Barnes & Noble)

2 4 6 8 10 9 7 5 3 1

Printed in China, May 2013.

Cocktails, Cocktails & more Cocktails

Kester Thompson

Photography by Danya Weiner

imagine!
Publishing

Contents

Introduction

The world of Cocktails can be mystifying and somewhat intimidating to say the least; never has so much fun been taken so seriously. It doesn't help that an unspoken hierarchy also seems to exist, whereby a good drink order gives you cool status, while a bad order gives you loser status. I think the problem is that indeed, many people do take their work very seriously. Now there's nothing wrong with that, but there is a fine balance between remembering that a cocktail is just a drink, and taking pride in your work, and then taking yourself way too seriously altogether. I firmly believe that pride and love are the two most important ingredients of any good cocktail, Cocktails are, first and foremost, about pleasure, a way of enjoying yourself – and if you don't enjoy yourself, then you're doing it wrong. The great Harry Craddock, author of the sacred Savoy Cocktail Book, once said that the way to drink a cocktail is quickly, "while it's still laughing at you." The thing is, the cocktail is not laughing at you, it's laughing with you.

The idea behind this particular book has always been to keep it simple. I've also tried to provide you with as many tips and alternatives and variations as I could think of, to help you try different methods or recipes. I know how I like to make drinks, and most of the recipes are based on that, but I've tried to alert you to other options wherever possible. Most of the drinks don't call for obscure or outrageously expensive ingredients, although once you start, you may find you want to experiment. And that brings me to the most important point. None of these recipes are set in stone – but then very few cocktail recipes are. For as much as bartenders love to claim that theirs is the proper way to make a drink, there are as many recipes out there for each drink as there are bartenders making them.

So, I urge you to try a recipe once, and then, as I do with cookery books, toss the book aside and make it your own, adapt it to your taste. However, here are some points to remember: First of all, always write down your changes – I promise you, you will not remember the following morning how you made the best cocktail in the world that you ended up drinking all night... Secondly, always measure carefully. The smallest amount more or less of an ingredient can change a drink. And thirdly, be consistent. Consistency is one of the main talents of a good bartender. Remember, it's just a drink. And in about two or three minutes, it will be gone, and you'll be feeling much better.

Glassware

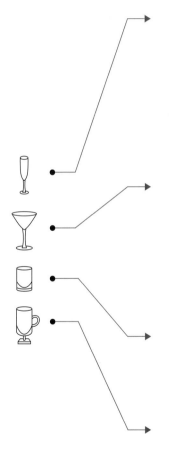

The "Must-Haves"

1. Champagne Flutes

5–6 oz should suffice. There are many varieties, but those with a hollow stem are a nightmare to clean. Champagne Saucers are not really suitable for Champagne, but they can serve as a nice alternative to a Cocktail glass.

2. Cocktail Glasses

also known as Martini glasses. The quintessential glass for cocktails, not too small and not too big. I personally favor a 7.5 oz size, with a brim that is not too wide Remember, the liquid must stay cold.

3. Collins

otherwise known as Highballs. If you can, get two sizes – one smaller, one larger (perhaps 9 oz and 12 oz).

4. Hot Drink

made from tempered glass, for hot drinks. You can always use a mug, but then you could serve oysters on a paper plate...

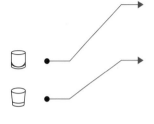

5. Old Fashioned

also known as Rocks, or Lo-ball.

6. Shot Glasses

again, endless styles. Don't go too small or too big – 2–3 oz. If you want to be really classy, find some stemmed, narrow Pousse Cafe glasses, which are far more elegant.

Great to Have the Option

7. Goblet

some recipes call for a Goblet, a wider, fatter take on a wine glass. They are impressive glasses.

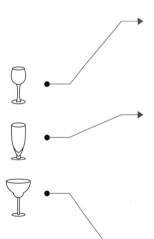

8. Hurricane

an hourglass shaped, stemmed glass, designed specifically for the cocktail of the same name. While the original is enormous, you can find smaller versions for drinks such as Piña Colada.

9. Margarita

for the obvious.

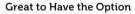

Necessary Equipment

Bar spoon

You can always use the spoons in your kitchen drawer, but once you start to use one, you'll find a bar spoon indispensable. Its long handle lends itself to all sorts of uses, such as measuring sugar, stirring, getting the last hard-to-reach olive out of the jar and so on. The handle's twisted groove comes in very handy when you're layering drinks. I prefer bar spoons with a flat disc at the top of the handle, as it helps when layering. If you get used to using only your bar spoon, you'll learn how to get consistent measurements, rather than having to adapt to every spoon you encounter.

Blender

If you've got one, great. If not, wait. A proper bar blender is not cheap. If you are using a bar blender, keep it well serviced and clean – there's nothing worse than a smelly blender. Try not to use it for ice cubes as they wear down the blades.

Channel Knife

Not to be confused with a zester, the channel knife cuts thin strips of citrus peel, known as twists, for use as garnish.

Extras

Cocktail sticks for garnishes

Napkins and coasters for serving drinks – cold glasses will frost over and drip.

Straws

Paper umbrellas – will not be required (or is it time for a comeback?!)

Bar cloth – ordinary kitchen tea towels don't polish glasses well and tend to smear.

Fine Strainer

This is one of my essential items. You can find a fine mesh, stainless steel strainer almost anywhere – you need one with a diameter of 4 inches – something like a fine tea strainer. A Hawthorn Strainer is essential if you're using a Boston Shaker (which you are, aren't you??), but it doesn't catch small pips, seeds, and tiny shards of ice, which can spoil the perfection of a drink served straight up.

Grater

At the very least you need a nutmeg grater, but a good grater will come in useful for all kinds of things.

Hawthorn Strainer

A generic trademark name for the strainer that fits onto the top of the Boston Shaker. The spring in the rim strains and also allows a bit of movement, should you wish to add solid ingredients to your drink.

Ice scoop

You'll waste an awful lot of time if you only work with a pair of ice tongs, taking one cube at a time. Cocktails use a lot of ice – a lot! – so an ice scoop is essential. A 6 oz one should be fine for home use.

Juicer

There are many types of juice extractors. A juicer is absolutely necessary – freshly squeezed juice doesn't come from a box, it comes from a piece of fruit that you squeeze by hand.

Knife (and cutting board)

You won't get anywhere without a good sharp knife and a board to cut on. A vegetable peeler is useful too.

Measures

I recommend buying a large variety of jiggers for measuring liquids, so you don't have to 'guesstimate.' You'll find that some jiggers have rather strange measurements – 1¼ oz being a popular one – which frankly are of little use. I also suggest that you have some measuring cups, big and small, as well as measuring spoons. I can't stress enough how important precision is with cocktails. It may be useful to know that an average bar spoon holds ⅛th of an ounce.

Mixing Glass

A glass vessel used for stirred cocktails. While you can always use the glass part of a Boston shaker, a good mixing glass gives you more room to work with. Besides, a good one looks so stylish. Make sure it fits your strainer...

Muddler

Muddling is the technical term for pressing / squashing / squeezing / crushing fruits and other non-liquid ingredients in your shaker. Any bar store will have a muddler. I recommend using a long one if possible, as the short ones are sometimes too short for the shaker. I personally use an old style rolling pin without handles. A rolling pin is also useful for making cracked and crushed ice. Wrap some ice in a towel, and imagine it's someone you really don't like.

Pourers

I would recommend getting some pourers for your bottles to help control the flow of liquid, but don't get the ones that have ball-bearings in and serve you a specific measure. Always replace the original bottle tops / corks / caps to prevent little winged creatures from drowning in your liqueur.

Shaker

I really urge you to get yourself a Boston Shaker. In my opinion the standard three part shakers, just don't do the job properly. A Boston shaker has two parts, a metal cone, and a glass part, or Boston glass. Shaken cocktails need to really be shaken, and a Boston shaker gives you plenty of room to smash those ingredients together.

Techniques & Terms

Building

Some drinks are delightfully simple, only requiring you pour the ingredients into the glass in the order given, with or without ice.

Chilling glasses

• It is always desirable to serve drinks straight up in a chilled or frosted glass. The simplest way to do this is to place the glass in the freezer well in advance.

• Barmen sometimes fill glasses with ice and water to chill them. While this may be a good emergency solution, it's not particularly stylish.

Double Straining

• When making drinks that are served straight up, with no ice, you may want to filter out any pips, seeds, small bits of mint leaf, and tiny shards of ice that the Hawthorn Strainer didn't catch. Pour the drink from the shaker, and still using the Hawthorn Strainer, hold a fine mesh strainer between the shaker and the glass, to catch any bits and pieces. You'll be surprised at what you may find.

• Sometimes your fine strainer gets clogged. Simply stir its contents with your bar spoon. This is also useful when you want to squeeze the very last drops out of ginger, or crushed strawberries, for example.

Garnishing

• Garnishing is the decorating of a drink. Always make sure your drink looks as beautiful as possible. It doesn't matter how much effort and love you put into it, if it looks unattractive it's not going to be appreciated as much as it should be, even if you know it tastes fantastic. Many drinks call for specific garnishes.

• If you want to improvise, try to match your garnish to the drink. For example, an olive would be out of place in a sweet, creamy cocktail.

• I like to make my garnishes edible wherever possible – and I certainly don't use anything that I wouldn't put in my mouth.

Infusing

• Infusing liqueurs with herbs, spices and other ingredients like fruit is a great way to experiment with other flavors, and more often than not, a homemade Vanilla Vodka, for example, will be much nicer than a commercially made one.

• Basically, you just put your ingredients into a bottle, close the cap tightly, and leave it for a few days.

• If you're using goods that can spoil, like some spices, herbs, or fruits, you must ensure that they are always covered by the liqueur. Vanilla Vodka is a good example. After you've used it a few times, the vanilla pod will poke out of the vodka and be exposed to air, causing it to decay. You can either a) remove the vanilla pod, b) transfer the liquid to another container, or c) add more vodka so that the vanilla is covered once more, although this will dilute the vanilla flavor.

• You can use a jar with an airtight seal for infusions.

• If you're 'steeping' fruits, I recommend using a jar with an airtight seal and leaving it in the refrigerator until it's ready. Once the liqueur has extracted all the flavor of the fruit, strain the liqueur and discard or eat the fruit. I recommend trying these flavors because they are easy to begin with: Cardamom / Chamomile / Chili – dried or fresh / Cinnamon Citrus peels – either one flavor or a mix / Coffee / Ginger / Nutmeg / Saffron / Sweet pepper / Vanilla.

• You can try these with any liqueur – it's entirely up to you.

• Some flavors are slightly bitter and you may want to add a touch of sugar – experiment.

Layering

• To layer drinks takes immense patience and concentration. I like to use a flat bottomed bar spoon. When layering one liquid on top of another, you first need to know whether it will float, so follow the recipes closely. Let the spoon rest on the surface of the liquid. Then, with your thumb over the top of the bottle or its pourer, let the contents dribble very slowly from the top of the twisted part of the spoon. Slowly! The liquid should spread itself over the surface of the base liquid. If it doesn't, and it mixes, you're either doing it too fast, or you've got the recipe wrong.

• For more information, see the section on Pousse Café (see page 130).

Measuring

• I assume that if you can read, you know how to measure ingredients. But let's just clarify a thing or two. I'll say this over and over and over... Measure precisely. A drink can be ruined by as little as a half teaspoon's worth of error.

• I'll also talk a lot about ratios. Many recipes (but not all – I would avoid recipes with very small measurements such as dashes, as the margin for error will, conversely, be greater) can be adapted for other measurements. If you don't have something for measuring fluid ounces or centiliters, you can use anything you want – a spoon, and bottle cap, whatever – as long as you stick to the proportional ratio. If a recipe calls for 1 oz of this, 1 oz of that, and 1 oz of the other, then you can even use a coffee cup to measure if you so desire. You may see many bartenders 'freepouring', or pouring without a measure. This takes a lot of practice and experience, and in the wrong hands it can be painfully inaccurate. Leave it for now... We'll tackle that another day.

Muddling

• A weird term, but an important one. I urge you to do all your muddling in the metal part of the shaker.

• Muddling basically means to squash, press and squeeze fruits, herbs, spices and other solid ingredients.

• Muddling fruits is obvious.

• Muddling a lime or a lemon with a muddling instrument is usually done with sugar. You're trying to squeeze all the juice out of the fruit, while the sugar works on the skin, extracting all the essential oils that are stored inside.

• When muddling herbs such as mint or basil, be very, very gentle. Press very lightly, don't squash. Many herbs release bitterness when squashed, and they discolor quickly. Don't get your face too close to the shaker when muddling. Getting lime juice, ginger, or chili in your eye will make you cry like a baby.

Shaking

• As a rule, cocktails that contain fruits, fruit juices, milk, cream, or eggs are shaken.

• To use a Boston Shaker – Put all your ingredients in the glass part of the shaker, and fill with ice. Cover with the metal part, tapping it firmly closed with the heel of your hand to create a seal. Turn the shaker upside down (so the glass part is on top), and with one hand on top and the other on the bottom, start shaking, while trying to look as cool as possible.

When you've finished shaking, hold the middle of the shaker in one hand, making sure you are gripping both parts. With the other hand, tap the edge of the metal where it covers the rim of the glass. This should break the seal, and you can lift the glass off, leaving the mixture in the metal part. If the seal doesn't break, turn the shaker in your hand and try again. I urge you to practice with an empty shaker. It can be a tad tricky to master – but it's worth the effort. You should shake a cocktail for about 20 seconds. Don't be afraid to use plenty of ice. In fact, basic physics states that the more ice you use, the quicker the drink will chill down, and the less ice will melt.

Why do we shake? One of the most important ingredients of nearly every cocktail is water. Approximately 25% of any cocktail is water in the form of melted ice, so this dilution is necessary. Shaking is the quickest way to simultaneously cool a drink while combining the ingredients. After 20 seconds the contents of the shaker are about as cold as they're going to get, and you should only shake longer when using eggs, or if you want to achieve a certain consistency with creamy drinks.

Stirring

As a rule, drinks that contain only alcoholic ingredients are stirred, because they blend easily without shaking. Moreover, shaking causes minute air bubbles to form and this can make a noticeable difference to the texture of the liquid. You'll hear talk of 'bruising' the liqueur (especially when it comes to Dry Martinis), and bartenders can argue endlessly about the merits of shaking versus stirring. Naturally it takes longer to chill a drink by stirring. I always stir my drinks 52 times, which is just under a minute, and it always seems to work for me.

To stir a drink you'll need a bar spoon. Some bartenders twiddle their bar spoon between finger and thumb, but I find it much easier to turn my bar spoon upside down, holding the bowl of the spoon, with the stem in the drink. As you stir, let the spoon work its way down to the bottom of the mixing glass by itself. Try not to agitate the ice too much – you want a nice smooth, gentle motion.

When stirring a cocktail, use a mixing glass. If you don't have one, the glass part of a Boston Shaker will suffice. You may see a 'stir and churn' instruction, in which case, you should agitate the ice. Stir and lift the spoon at the same time to churn the ingredients together.

Straining

To strain a drink after you've shaken or stirred, place your Hawthorn Strainer firmly over the top of the shaker or mixing glass, using your index finger and middle finger. Hold the shaker firmly and strain. Again, practice makes perfect.

Sugar or Salt Rim

Some recipes require you to coat the rim of a glass with salt or sugar. This can be done by moistening the rim of the glass with a piece of lemon or lime, for example, and then gently dipping the glass into a plate of sugar or salt. It is best to hold the glass horizontally, turning it slightly after each dip, so that the rim is coated but there are no crystals inside the glass.

Twists

There are basically three types of twist – that I use, anyway. Twists are strips of citrus peel that can be used for decoration, or to add an extra kick to a drink. The oils packed within the skin of a nice firm citrus fruit are powerfully aromatic, delightfully tasty and bitter, and they can make an ordinary drink fantastic. When the oil from a twist is sprayed onto a drink, the smell will reach your nose before you even taste the cocktail. The oil is also very flammable, and some cocktails call for lighting the oil as you spray it onto the drink... More to follow.

The first kind of twist is made with a channel knife, which will give you a long thin strip of citrus peel. These twists are mainly decorative. Tie them in a knot, or curl one around a straw and press it, and you'll get a delightfully kitschy citrus coil to drape over the rim of a glass.

The second is more serious... Using a vegetable peeler, cut a strip of peel from the top to the bottom of the fruit, while holding the fruit over the drink, so as to catch any oil that is expressed as you cut. Another way is more difficult, but I prefer it.

• Cut the top and bottom off the fruit. Stand the fruit on its cut base and cut a good slice of peel from top to bottom.
• The pith is ugly and bitter, and must be trimmed off. Lay the twist, pith up, on a flat surface, and use a knife to trim the pith from the twist – like skinning a fish... Just watch your fingers!!
• Straighten the edges of the twist with your knife. Holding the twist over the drink between your middle finger and thumb, gently apply pressure so it bends in on itself. You should be able to see the oil spraying onto the drink. Twist it every way possible – but gently – to express every last drop of oil without tearing it. Now rub the skin side of the twist around the rim of the glass, so that the oil is tasted with every mouthful.
• Curl the twist and drop it in the drink.

Third – to 'flame a twist'... Cut a slice of peel from the fruit (make sure it's good and oily) – not a long strip, but more of a circle. Make your cut as close to the skin as possible so there's not too much pith – and definitely no flesh. Using a cigarette lighter (I prefer lighters to matches, and always a butane lighter – never a gasoline lighter, or your drink will taste like an engine) and holding the twist between forefinger and thumb of your non-lighter hand, gently warm the twist over the flame for a couple of seconds.
• Hold the twist over the drink, not straight down, but at a 45° angle (or you'll burn yourself). Hold the lighter in front of the twist above the drink, and squeeze the twist to express the oil through the flame onto the surface of the drink. Yes, you'll get a surprise. Yes, you'll get black smoke, and dirty fingers, and yes you'll get black, burnt oil on the surface of the drink. And yes, it will taste extraordinary!

Ingredients

As with cooking, the better your ingredients,
the better your cocktail will be. Some quick tips...

Bitters

Many recipes call for bitters, more specifically Angostura Bitters, which are widely available. There are all kinds of cocktail bitters out there, and Angostura are perhaps the best known. They are highly concentrated, so you will only ever need a dash or two to make a difference. Most bitters have secret recipes – only five people know the exact recipe for Angostura Bitters – so I can't really tell you what's in them. If you like bitters it can be a fascinating avenue to explore.

Eggs

• Eggs are an essential component of several cocktails. Egg white emulsifies a cocktail, binding the ingredients and providing a super smooth, frothy texture, without leaving any taste. You don't have to use them, but it will change the drink.

• When using eggs, I recommend giving the cocktail a 'dry shake' first, in other words shake without ice, to let the egg do its work without having to worry about the time pressure of melting ice. Then add the ice and shake again.

Fresh Juices

• Freshly squeezed means freshly squeezed, not squeezed, put in a carton with additives, and placed on a shelf. If you're making drinks for yourself there's absolutely no reason why you shouldn't squeeze juices as you make your cocktails.

• Lemon and lime juices are essential. By the way, they are not one and the same. They have very distinct flavors and qualities. To prepare in advance, squeeze the juice, strain it, and transfer it to a clean, empty bottle or container.

• If you must buy apple or pineapple juice, go for the freshest, most natural versions you can find. It really does make a difference.

Ice

• Make sure your ice is clean, fresh and cold, and as 'dry' as possible (i.e. as close to frozen as possible.)

• Denser ice cubes are preferable, as opposed to the hollow ice cubes produced by some freezers and ice machines. Denser ice melts more slowly, while hollow ice will dilute your drink too much.

• Find out whether your water has a high mineral content, and if this gives your ice a taste. Perhaps use filtered water.

• For crushed ice, you can buy an ice crusher, or else wrap your ice in a tea towel and smash it with a flat, wooden kitchen mallet or rolling pin. It's a great way to work off anger...

Liqueur and Alcohol

I have no intention of steering you towards particular brands, except in those cases where I firmly believe that a specific product has a unique taste. But remember that cheap liqueur can kill a drink and destroy its taste, as well as leaving you with a hangover the next day. On the other hand, very expensive ingredients are simply wasted if mixed with other ingredients. You know what you can afford, and I will leave it to your discretion to pick out your brands.

Sugar

There will be much talk of sugar in the following pages and whether it is preferable to use granulated, superfine, or brown sugars or sugar syrup. Sugar syrup is the most user-friendly. I have also noted where you should use actual sugar.

Sugar Syrup

The endless arguments about how to make a decent sugar syrup revolve around the sugar to water ratio. I suggest you experiment for yourself, although I personally favor a 2 sugar: 1 water ratio. Heat water in a pan, add double the amount of sugar, and stir until thoroughly dissolved, without letting it boil. You can also experiment with Demerara or Turbinado sugar. The most important thing is to always stick to your ratio, otherwise your recipes will be off kilter. Refrigerate.

Preparation

- You should always be well prepared before you start making a cocktail.
- Make sure your glass is ready.
- Make sure you have all the necessary equipment.
- Prepare your garnish.
- Prepare any ice you may need.
- Make sure you have all your ingredients ready (less obvious than it sounds!).
- When you start pouring, it's best to add the cheapest ingredients first, in case of any mistakes.
- Once the ice goes into the shaker, your time is limited.
- As soon as you've finished shaking, quickly taste the contents by dipping a straw into the shaker, covering the top of the straw with your finger, putting the dipped end in your mouth and releasing your finger from the top. You can still adjust your cocktail while it's in the shaker – you can't once it's in the glass.
- Pour the drink as quickly as possible.
- Don't get upset if the cocktail doesn't taste right , IT'S JUST A DRINK!
- Pour it out, start again, and try to figure out what went wrong.
- The most important thing is to have fun.

Recipes

Mixed Drinks

01

Mixed Drinks

Mixed
Drinks

Most of the Mixed Drinks in this chapter go back a long way, in fact I would guess that most modern bartenders don't know much about them. So why am I including them here, you may ask? First of all, I personally find these drinks of great interest and importance, but more importantly, they are fairly simple to make, and they don't require a whole lot of ingredients - meaning they are a tasty way to get to know your ingredients, and to experiment with whatever you've got to hand.

As you go through the various types or families, you'll notice, as I'll try and point out, that many of them are very similar – almost identical. But also, try to see how these recipes may have evolved into modern drinks that you already know. I've been somewhat ruthless with my choices, as it would take an entire book to go through all these old Mixed Drinks, so if I've left out something that you think I shouldn't have, well, I hope you can forgive me. Most of the Mixed Drinks can be made with most liqueurs, and in many cases wines, including champagne, sherry, port and madeira.

Sherry Cobbler

GLASS
Goblet or Collins

The perfect way to start us off and the very height of simplicity. The Cobbler is mentioned as early as 1844 in Charles Dickens' Martin Chuzzlewit, and indeed a 'Cobler' is referred to in an article written by Edgar Allen Poe, in Burton's Gentlemen's Magazine, 1837. Cobblers can be made with a whole range of liqueurs, and also wines (there are recipes for claret, hock, champagne etc).

Ingredients
4 oz / 12 cl dry sherry *
2 bar spoons superfine sugar
1 orange slice **
2 pineapple chunks **

Preparation
• Roughly muddle the fruits in the base of the shaker. **
• Add the other ingredients and shake together quickly with cracked or crushed ice.
• Pour contents into the glass, adding more ice if necessary.
• Garnish with lots of seasonal fruits.
• Serve with a straw. ***

Tips
* I would stick with one of the drier sherries – Fino, Amontillado, Manzanilla, or perhaps, if you want a richer drink, Oloroso.
** This is optional. Maybe you'll like it, or perhaps you prefer the cleaner taste of sherry by itself.
*** Straw is essential, and I also use a long handled dessert spoon to reach all the fruit.

Cherry Cobbler

GLASS
Goblet or Collins

A great drink, although the addition of lemon juice is unusual.

Ingredients
2 oz / 6 cl gin
1 oz / 3 cl Cherry Heering or cherry brandy
½ bar spoon superfine sugar
½ oz / 1½ cl freshly squeezed lemon juice

Preparation
• Dissolve the sugar in the glass with the lemon juice.
• Add ice, followed by the rest of the ingredients, ending with the gin.
• Stir well until the glass is frosted.
• Garnish with lots of seasonal fruit.
• Serve with a straw.

The Cobbler was perhaps the first drink that required the use of a straw, and while to us, a straw is something we barely notice, back in the time of Martin Chuzzlewit, they were utterly strange, and required explanation, as Dickens takes great pleasure in describing. Is it just a coincidence that the common three-part cocktail shaker appeared in the late 19th Century, at the height of Cobbler fame, and is known as a Cobbler shaker? (Robert Hess suggests that a "Cobler" is an old name for a brewer or innkeeper). The recipes are very simple – basically a liqueur, with sugar, ice and fruit. However, the last two ingredients are key.

Whisky Cobbler

Glass

Goblet or Collins

Ingredients

2 oz / 6 cl whisky – your choice

1 bar spoon superfine white sugar

1 bar spoon Maraschino liqueur
  (optional)

1 bar spoon Grand Marnier or
  Cointreau (optional)

1 orange slice (optional)

Preparation

**If you're including the orange
slice and /or other fruits:**

• Muddle the orange in the base
of the shaker.

• Add other ingredients and shake
together quickly with cracked
or crushed ice.

• Pour contents into the glass,
adding more ice if necessary

• Garnish with lots of
seasonal fruits.

• Serve with a straw.

**If you're not including the
orange slice:**

• Dissolve sugar in the glass with
a dash of water.

• Add ice and the rest of the
ingredients, ending with
the whisky.

• Stir well until the glass is frosted.

• Garnish with lots of seasonal fruit.

• Serve with a straw.

Whisky Cocktail

Glass
Cocktail (if served straight up) or Old Fashioned (if served with ice)

In his 1862 Bartender's Guide Jerry Thomas lists several cocktail recipes, including whisky, brandy, vermouth and champagne, and they follow this recipe, with the inclusion of ice (as a form of water). What is interesting to me is that he also lists the Manhattan Cocktail, and later Harry Johnson, in 1882, lists a Martini Cocktail. His Manhattan, which is pretty much the same today, as you will see, calls for Maraschino or Curaçao (as a sweetener in place of sugar), whisky and vermouth (liqueur), bitters and ice (water). Johnson's recipe for Martini Cocktail is sugar syrup, bitters, Old Tom gin and vermouth, and ice. The Manhattan, the forerunner of the (not yet Dry) Martini, the Old Fashioned, the Sazerac, and perhaps even the Mint Julep (although there is a separate Julep family) all follow this simple recipe to some degree. I could go on for a long while, but perhaps it would be more interesting for you to mix a cocktail and contemplate its influence.

The ingredients of cocktails are liqueur, sugar, water and bitters. It's as simple as that.

Ingredients
2 oz / 6 cl rye whisky or bourbon
3 dashes sugar syrup – no more than one teaspoonful
2 Angostura Bitters *
1-2 dashes of Curaçao (such as Cointreau) (optional)

Preparation
Either
• Stir ingredients in a mixing glass 52 times.
Or
• Shake ingredients with ice.
Then
• Double strain into a chilled cocktail glass, or strain into an Old Fashioned with ice.
• Garnish with a cocktail cherry and a lemon twist (spray oil over the drink and wipe around the rim of the glass). **

Tips
* The original bitters used were Boker's Bitters, which are hard to find. Angostura will do fine.
** I personally prefer an orange twist.

Optional
• Improved Whisky Cocktail (Jerry Thomas) – Add a couple of dashes of Maraschino liqueur and a dash of absinthe.

═══ **Variations** ═══
As I wrote earlier, Jerry Thomas offers several variations, including brandy, vermouth (Sweet), gin (both Jenever and Old Tom), absinthe, champagne, and a coffee cocktail (made with port, brandy and a whole egg – no coffee), a Jersey cocktail (made with applejack), and a Japanese cocktail (basically a brandy cocktail sweetened with orgeat or almond syrup).

Brandy Crusta

Glass

Small Wine Glass or whatever you prefer!

To garnish a Crusta, first coat the rim of your glass with sugar. Then take a lemon (some say orange, and that variation works for me), cut off both ends, and peel the skin away in one piece – whether you use a sharp knife or a vegetable peeler is up to you, tidiness is not an issue, and as it happens, the more rustic it looks the better. The lemon peel should line the inside of the glass and poke out of the top, as if offering a second rim to drink from. The sugar rim not only adds taste, but it helps hold the thing in place. I cannot emphasize enough that you must coat the rim in sugar beforehand, and chill the glass in the fridge to form a sugar crust, or you'll get some horrible sugar-and-peel sliding action, which can be infuriating.

Ingredients

2 oz brandy

1 bar spoon Cointreau

1 bar spoon Maraschino liqueur
(optional)

1 bar spoon freshly squeezed
lemon juice

½ – 1 bar spoon sugar syrup

1 – 2 dashes of Angostura Bitters

Preparation

• Prepare the glass as
instructed above.

• Shake the ingredients with ice.

• Double strain into glass.

Tips

• You can play around with
the measures of Cointreau,
Maraschino, sugar and lemon to
get the right balance of sweet
and sour. But be restrained –
amounts should be kept to
a minimum.

• Harry Johnson mentions using
something called Orchard Syrup.
It has been suggested that it
might be some kind of apple cider
syrup, which, if true, could be
very nice!

Brandy Daisy à la Jerry Thomas

Glass
Cocktail or Old Fashioned

Ingredients
2 oz / 6 cl brandy
1 bar spoon Cointreau
1 bar spoon of sugar syrup
½ oz / 1½ cl freshly squeezed
   lemon juice
1 bar spoon Jamaican rum
   (such as Myers's)
Top off with soda water
   (from a siphon if possible)

Optional
• Harry Johnson omits the
Cointreau and rum, replacing
them with about ½ oz / 1½ cl
yellow Chartreuse, and
garnishing with seasonal fruit.
• For a whisky or gin Daisy
Thomas omits the Curaçao, or
Cointreau, and adds about ½ bar
spoon of orgeat.

Preparation
• Shake ingredients
(except the soda) with ice.
• Strain into a chilled glass.
• Top off with soda water
(don't overdo it).

Whisky Daisy adapted from Harry Johnson

Glass
Old Fashioned

These old Mixed Drinks can drive you crazy. Take a look at any Daisy recipe, and you'll never find two the same – and to make matters worse, they tend to vary yet again when you change the base liqueur. We're not talking small changes like a dash here or there, we're talking significant ingredients! Daisies probably originated in the first half of the 19th Century. Many recipes call for grenadine syrup (pomegranate) as a sweetener. Jerry Thomas uses sugar and Curaçao, or sugar and orgeat (depending on the liqueur), while Harry Johnson uses sugar and yellow Chartreuse.

Ingredients
2 oz / 6 cl brandy
½ oz / 1½ cl Yellow Chartreuse
1 bar spoon of sugar
½ oz / 1½ cl freshly squeezed
   lemon juice
1 dash of soda water

Preparation
• Dissolve the sugar in the soda
water in the glass part of
the shaker.
• Add the rest of the ingredients
and stir together well.
• Strain into a glass filled with
crushed ice.
• Garnish with seasonal fruit.
• Strain into a glass with
crushed ice.

Gin Fix

Gin Fizz

Glass
Old Fashioned

Glass
Small Collins

A Fix is similar to a Daisy or a smaller Cobbler with citrus. They're almost unheard of in today's bars. Essentially they are liqueur sweetened with sugar and / or Curaçao and / or a fruit syrup, such as raspberry or pineapple.

The Fizz is often confused with a Collins. A good Fizz should be made, served, and drunk quickly. Harry Johnson says of the Silver Fizz: "This drink is a delicious one, and must be drank (sic) as soon as prepared, as it loses its strength and flavor." Here is a modern recipe for Gin Fizz (yes, you can use any liqueur), with some variations.

Ingredients

1 bar spoon superfine sugar
   dissolved in a little water
2 oz / 6 cl gin
   (Jenever, Old Tom, or Dry)
½ oz / 1½ cl freshly squeezed
   lemon juice
1 bar spoon raspberry syrup or
   pineapple syrup

Preparation

• Mix ingredients in a glass with ice.
• Garnish with seasonal berries.

Tip

• You can play with the measures
to get a balance of sweet and sour.

Ingredients

2 oz / 6 cl gin
   (Jenever, Old Tom or Dry)
1 bar spoon superfine sugar
¾ – 1 oz freshly squeezed
   lemon juice
Top off with soda water

Preparation

• Dissolve the sugar in the shaker
with lemon juice.
• Add the gin and shake with ice.
• Strain into a chilled glass without
ice and top off with soda water.

Variations

**Silver Fizz – add one egg white.
Don't be squeamish, it's an
excellent drink.
Golden Fizz – add one egg yolk.
Sloe Gin Fizz – A truly
scrumptious drink, well worth
buying a bottle of sloe gin.
Ginger Fizz – substitute ginger
ale for the soda water.
Ramos Gin Fizz – see page 59.**

Boston Flip

Glass
Cocktail Glass or Flute

This is one of my favorite versions of a Flip, although it requires madeira, which is not a common ingredient.

Ingredients
1½ oz / 4½ cl bourbon or rye
1½ oz / 4½ cl Madeira
1 egg
1 bar spoon superfine sugar

Preparation
• Shake ingredients without ice.
• Shake again with ice.
• Strain into a chilled glass and
• Sprinkle with grated nutmeg.

Tips
• If you want to try before you buy, use Port instead of Madeira, although I would reduce the amount. It's not the same, but will provide a similar richness to the drink.
• Modern recipes often include a splash of heavy cream. It's up to you – although it's bordering dangerously on Eggnog territory.
• I also recommend applejack, brandy, or Jamaican rum.
• Another great recipe is the Chocolate Flip. There's no chocolate but it uses equal measures of brandy and sloe gin and a splash of cream... Mmmmmmm.
• If you want to serve it hot, you may want to use a different glass.

Flips are a very old form of Mixed Drinks. The original Flips were based on ale and heated with a red hot poker. Flips can be served cold or hot and can be made with a whole array of base liqueurs and wines. They are a great winter drink. Some say that only the yolk of an egg should be used, but I don't think this is right.

Eggnog

Glass
Collins, or Old Fashioned (or Mug if hot)

This is the original 19th Century version, although I'm using Jamaican rum, rather than Santa Cruz.

Ingredients
1½ oz / 4½ cl brandy
1 oz / 3 cl Jamaican rum
1 egg
2 – 3 oz / 6 – 9cl Half and Half cream
1 bar spoon superfine sugar

Preparation
• Shake ingredients without ice.
• Shake again with ice.
• Strain into a chilled glass and sprinkle with grated nutmeg.

Tips
• I'm sure you can think of a way to heat it up – just don't boil it, or it will be ruined. If you like eggnog, you can experiment with all kinds of liqueurs. Don't be afraid to use liqueurs and wines such as Madeira, peach liqueur etc. for extra flavor.

Eggnog is also a very old drink, going back several hundred years in England, and probably arriving in America sometime in the 18th Century. A proper Eggnog is very similar to a Flip (while there is one basic Eggnog, there are also variations), except that Eggnog contains milk. When made well it is delicious hot or cold.

Gin Rickey

Glass
Collins

Ingredients
1½–2 oz / 4½–6 cl gin
½ lime

Preparation
• Top off with soda water.
• Put ice in the glass.
• Squeeze the juice of the lime into the glass and add the spent shell.
• Add the gin and top off with soda water.

Colonel Joe Rickey, a Civil War veteran of Fulton, Missouri, and a regular of, and by some accounts a later owner of the legendary Shoomaker's Bar in Washington D.C.. He was very fond of drinking his whisky with carbonated water. Anyhow, the story goes that Rickey, with the help of George A. Williamson, the bartender, experimented adding lime juice to his bourbon and soda, the final recipe being the juice of half a lime with the shell thrown in for good measure. Thus the Rickey was born. Its lack of sugar was the key, with just the right amount of sour lime to make it ultimately refreshing.

Frisco Sour

Glass
Sour or Cocktail

Ingredients
1½ oz / 4½ cl bourbon or rye
½ oz / 1½ cl Benedictine
½ oz / 1½ cl freshly squeezed lemon juice

Preparation
• Shake ingredients with ice.
• Double strain into a chilled glass.
• Garnish with a twist of lemon.

Optional
The above is a fairly standard version, but I really like this version from Jay Hepburn:
   2 oz / 6 cl bourbon
   1 oz / 3 cl Benedictine
   ½ oz / 1½ cl freshly squeezed lemon juice
   ¼ oz / ¾ cl freshly squeezed lime juice

I personally love using egg whites in Sours. It acts as an homogenizing, emulsifying agent, giving you a smoother, beautifully frothy, almost creamy texture. If you do decide to use egg whites, test different quantities, changing the balance of sweet and sour. You don't have to use expensive liqueur, but have plenty of fresh lemons, and make sure you use the same sugar syrup at all times. Have fun!

Highballs

Highballs

The Highball only came into being in 1895, according to its creator, New York barman Patrick Gavin Duffy. However, the British were adding soda water to brandy way before then, since soda water had been commercially available since the late 18th Century.

A Highball is any kind of liqueur mixed with a non-alcoholic mixer and ice – served, obviously in a Highball (or a Collins if you prefer). Originally the mixers were carbonated (soda or tonic waters) but later fruit juices were also used. While the ratio is entirely up to the drinker, or rather the person pouring, a Highball should be no more than a 3:1 ratio (between 2-3 is best).

Here are some old and new ideas for you... All are served in a Highball or Collins, with ice, unless otherwise specified.

Brandy and Ginger Ale
A great, simple mixed drink. Don't knock it till you've tried it.

Cuba Libre
From Cuba, c.1900, White Cuban rum and Coca Cola, with a few squeezed wedges of lime thrown in for good measure.

Souq G&T
While it's impossible to improve on a good old G&T, here is my variation: Hendricks gin and tonic water, garnished with 2 long cucumber strips, orange and lemon slices, 3 chives, a sprig of dill, and a long green / spring onion or scallion to stir. You can stir (or even use as a straw).

Sea Breeze
Technically a Highball? Hmmm... Not really (I believe a Highball with two mixers must contain one carbonated), but what the heck. Try the layered version:
• Pour 2 oz / 6 cl cranberry juice into a glass with ice.
• Shake 2 oz / 6 cl vodka and 1½ oz / 4½ cl freshly squeezed grapefruit juice with ice.
• Strain carefully over the ice so it forms a layer on top of the cranberry juice.

Pepper or Chili Vodka with Freshly Pressed Pineapple Juice
Seriously, it's amazing

Zubrowka Bison Grass Vodka and Freshly Pressed Apple Juice
Another of my all time favorite drinks

My Zubrowka Sour

Glass
Cocktail

I'm sure there are a million versions of this,
but I'm ignoring them...

Ingredients

2 oz / 6 cl Zubrowka Bison
    Grass vodka

1 oz / 3 cl freshly pressed
    apple juice

1 oz / 3 cl freshly squeezed
    lime juice

½ oz / 1½ cl sugar syrup

A splash of elderflower cordial
    (optional)

½ of one egg white

Preparation

• Shake ingredients without ice.

• Shake again with ice.

• Double strain into a chilled glass.

• Sprinkle grated nutmeg over
the top.

The basic ingredients of a Sour are liqueur (almost anything goes these days, including liqueurs), lemon or lime juice, and sugar in some form. The inclusion of bitters and egg white is an area of much debate. The ratio of liqueur: lemon: sugar, is usually 2:1:1, or 4:2:1, 8:3:4 (more sugar than lemon), or even 2:2:1. This balancing of sweet and sour in relation to the base liqueur is one of the main techniques in cocktail making. It differs from drink to drink, ingredient to ingredient, brand to brand, lemon to lemon.

Whisky Sour

Glass
Old Fashioned (just my choice)

Ingredients

2 oz / 6 cl bourbon or rye

1 oz / 3 cl freshly squeezed
    lemon juice

¾ oz / 2¼ cl sugar syrup

½ of one egg white

Preparation

• Shake ingredients without ice.

• Shake again with ice.

• Strain into a chilled glass
without ice.

• Garnish with cocktail cherry and orange slice.*

• Drink while the ingredients are still married.

Tip

* I really like the Jerry Thomas garnish of berries – a seasonal thing. Irish whisky is also very popular for Sours.

Who knows where the Sour originates? Its first appearance is in Jerry Thomas's 1862 Edition, but it must be older than that, and it's not a huge step away from a Crusta or a Daisy. The Whisky Sour, perhaps the patriarch of the family, is the official drink of the illustrious Jefferson Literary and Debating Society of Virginia University which was founded in 1825, although no one knows if it made an appearance at the inaugural meeting.

Whisky Sour

Vodka & Gin Cocktails

02

Vodka
&
Gin

Cocktails

The name Vodka is believed to come from the Slavic word for water, voda; the 'k' is a suffix, making it 'little water.' Interestingly, this gives it a connection to the name Aqua Vitae (water of life), an archaic term for distilled spirits, that is today more specifically used in the translated names of Akvavit, Eau de Vie. Incidentally, both the names whisky and whiskey (depending on where it is made) also find their origin in the Gaelic and Irish for Aqua Vitae. Vodka is most commonly made from grains such as wheat, rye or corn, although you can distill it from just about any plant matter rich in starch. I am personally a big fan of potato vodkas, which are primarily produced in Poland. Whichever brand you choose, just don't let yourself be seduced by a glossy advertisement. At the same time, don't go too cheap. There are some truly bad vodkas out there, containing a lot of impurities that not only taste terrible, but will leave you feeling the same way.

I must immediately confess a conflict of interest – I love gin. For me, a good Gin & Tonic with a squeezed wedge of fresh lime is about as close to perfection as a drink can get. Gin is made like vodka, from distilled grains, but it is the addition of juniper and other botanicals and spices that makes gin endlessly fascinating, complex, and refreshing.

Bloody Mary Simple (Purist) Recipe

Glass

Collins

Ingredients

2 oz / 6 cl vodka

4 oz / 12 cl tomato juice

1 dash of freshly squeezed
    lemon juice

4–5 dashes of Worcestershire
    Sauce *

4–6 drops of Tabasco Pepper
    Sauce

1 pinch of celery salt

1–2 pinches of cracked black
    pepper

*** I strongly recommend using Lea
& Perrins Worcestershire Sauce**

Preparation

• (Optional) rim the glass with salt,
celery salt and black pepper.

• Pour the ingredients together
with ice from one half of the
shaker to the other about
10 times.

• Strain into a glass with ice.

• Garnish with a stick of celery.

Optional

People use a variety of ingredients
in their Bloody Mary's. It is simply
a question of personal taste.
Here are some optional
extras, should you feel like
experimenting:

• a dash of Dry or Sweet Sherry
  or Port

• ½ teaspoon of freshly grated
  or creamed horseradish
  (the latter mixes more easily)

• salt

• cayenne pepper

• muddled sweet pepper

• freshly blended tomatoes
  instead of tomato juice

• V8 or something similar instead
  of tomato juice

• I sometimes add a dash of demi-
  glace to give it a rich, meaty
  flavor

Tips

• Go easy on the ingredients.
You can always stir in more of
your favorites to make it spicier
once you've tasted it...

• Celery salt may be hard to find,
but it is well worth the trouble.

Like so many of the great classics, the origin and recipe of this perfect
brunch drink / hangover cure are still argued over. Most believe that
the Bloody Mary, which has also, at various times, gone by the names
The Bucket of Blood and The Red Snapper, was invented by Fernand
'Pete' Petiot, at the New York Bar, Paris, in 1921 or thereabouts. The
Bloody Mary is a very personal thing, and the range of possible
ingredients you sometimes see these days is staggering. I would urge
you to start simply – especially if you're making these for guests – and
develop your recipe over time, testing out new additions as you go
along, rather than all at once.

Variations

Red Snapper
replace the vodka with gin

Bloody Maria
replace the vodka with tequila

Bloody Joseph
replace the vodka with whiskey

Virgin Mary **or** Bloody Shame
with no alcohol

Bloody Caesar
with clamato juice instead
if tomato juice

Bloody Bull
with beef consommé instead
of tomato juice

Bull Shot
with beef bouillon instead of
tomato juice

Bloody Mary

Cosmopolitan

Glass

Cocktail

Despite many claims of authorship, we will never really know where the drink came from. However, the Cosmo it is often closely associated with Dale DeGroff (a.k.a. the King of Cocktails), the godfather of the modern New York cocktail scene, who formalized the recipe in the mid 90's, before it was picked up by Carrie Bradshaw and Co. in 1998. There are many variations to the recipe, and I've tried most, but this is the one that has served me best over the years.

Ingredients

1½ oz / 4½ cl citrus vodka

1 oz / 3 cl Cointreau

1 oz / 3 cl freshly squeezed
    lime juice

1½ oz / 4½ cl cranberry juice

Preparation

• Shake ingredients with ice.

• Double strain into a chilled glass.

• Flame an orange twist over the top of the drink, wipe around the rim of the glass, and drop inside.

Tips

• Make sure you use good quality cranberry juice.

• It's hard to find, but a few drops of orange bitters really gives a Cosmo a lift.

• If you find the drink a bit harsh, change the recipe to 2 oz / 6cl of cranberry juice.

Optional

Try out other recipes, which all differ slightly – even if just to see how such a well known drink can appear in so many different forms. Many advocate the use of Rose's lime cordial, although I heartily disagree.

Recommendations

• Try adding a piece of muddled fresh ginger to make a **Ginger Cosmopolitan.**

• I like to swap cranberry juice for the equally sour but deeper tasting freshly pressed pomegranate juice, which is harder to find, but excellent.

• Try both of the above together. It may not exactly be a Cosmopolitan, but I love it.

Variations

You can substitute citrus vodka for other flavored vodkas to create new tastes – for example if you use a blackcurrant or raspberry flavored vodka you get a Metropolitan. **The London NYC Hotel created the** London Sexy **version of the Cosmopolitan, using cardamom-infused vodka and a few mint leaves for a Middle Eastern twist. If you substitute Grand Marnier for Cointreau, you have a** Grand Cosmopolitan. **Top off the glass with a dash of champagne to make a** Royal Cosmopolitan.

Cosmopolitan

Espresso Martini

Glass
Cocktail

This is another drink that appears in various guises, each with a different name — Vodka Espresso, Pharmaceutical Stimulant, etc. This is my version.

Ingredients

1 oz / 3 cl vodka
1 oz / 3 cl vanilla vodka
1 dash of Kahlua
1 dash of Amaretto
½ oz / 1½ cl sugar syrup
1 freshly made double espresso*

* Note – it's called Espresso Martini, not Instant Coffee or Percolated Coffee Martini...

Preparation

• Shake ingredients very well with a lot of ice.
• Double strain into a chilled glass.
• Garnish with grated nutmeg or a few coffee beans.

Tips

• I have never seen anyone drink more than two of these and retain any shred of dignity.... With a good dose of alcohol and a double espresso, this is a potent drink!
• Try to make and serve this drink quickly. The espresso should be freshly made. Use a lot of ice and a really good shake so as not to over-dilute. If you've shaken it well, it should almost have the appearance of Guinness when poured.

Optional

• You don't have to use Kahlua and Amaretto, but I really think they add to the drink. At least try to use Kahlua, and think of the Amaretto as the almond icing on the cake.
• This drink can also be served in a rocks glass on ice, although I prefer it straight up in a cocktail glass.

Variations

I sometimes make this drink with strong Turkish coffee and cardamom instead of double espresso, which can give it a really interesting twist. Make sure you strain the coffee really well to avoid getting sludge in the bottom of your glass. Alternatively, just use cardamom-infused vodka instead of regular vodka, and follow the recipe above.

Espresso Martini

French Martini

Glass
Cocktail

A delightfully simple cocktail, easy on both the eye and the palate. The French part of the name comes from the use of the very decadent Chambord (Royal Chambord Liqueur), a rather expensive, but excellent black raspberry liqueur.

Ingredients

2 oz / 6 cl vodka
½ oz / 1½ cl Chambord Liqueur
2 oz / 6 cl freshly pressed
    pineapple juice

Preparation

• Shake ingredients with ice.
• Double strain into a chilled glass.
• Garnish with a wedge of pineapple.

Tips

• If you don't have Chambord you can also get good results with either Crème de Mure (blackberry liqueur) or Crème de Framboise (raspberry liqueur).
• If you really must, canned pineapple juice will give you an OK drink, but as always, try to find freshly pressed, or even better, press a pineapple yourself. Just don't use canned pineapple chunks!

Melon Martini

Glass
Cocktail

Perhaps the most popular of all the Fruit Martinis. It is naturally colorful and sweet (but not sickly sweet), and the only problem is the speed at which you'll find yourself drinking them.

Melon Martini #1

Ingredients
2 oz / 6 cl vodka
½ oz / 1½ cl sugar syrup
Flesh of ⅛ - ⅙ melon, without
    seeds

Preparation
• Muddle the melon in the base of a shaker.
• Add the other ingredients and shake with ice.
• Double strain into a chilled glass.
• Garnish with a slice of melon.

Tips
Choose your melon carefully. Some options are:
Canary: nicely sweet and tangy, but lacks vivid color.
Cantaloupe: less sweet, but has a delightful orange hue, so try not to use any green ingredients.
Honeydew: sweet and juicy, and nice and green.
Santa Claus: while slightly lacking in color, very sweet, and perfect for a Christmas drink.

Melon Martini #2

Ingredients
2 oz / 6 cl vodka
1 oz / 3 cl melon schnapps or
    liqueur (such as Midori)
¼–½ oz / ¾-1½ cl sugar syrup

Preparation
• Shake all the ingredients and shake with ice.
• Double strain into a chilled glass.
• Garnish with a slice of melon.

Tip
If your cocktail is a little too sweet try adding a squeeze of fresh lime.

There are two basic methods to making Fruit Martinis: one natural, the other with liqueurs:
• The first method uses fresh fruits and ingredients wherever possible, and for this reason I like to call them Market Martinis.

• The second method involves a mixture of fruit juices and liqueurs, or schnapps, or sometimes syrups. The advantage is that, if you stick to your favorite brands, you will get the same result every time, which is a big bonus if you're entertaining guests – and to my mind, consistency is one of the main attributes of a good bartender.

Cucumber Martini

Glass

Cocktail

Cucumber is not an everyday drink ingredient, but on a summer afternoon this can be a very pleasant and delightfully delicate thirst-quencher.

Cucumber Martini #1

Ingredients

2 oz vodka

½ oz / 1½ cl sugar syrup

2½ inches / 6 cm chopped
   cucumber

Preparation

• Muddle the cucumber in the
base of the shaker.

• Add the rest of the ingredients
and shake with ice.

• Double strain into a chilled glass.

• Garnish with a cucumber spiral,
or a long slice of cucumber.

Tip

Cucumber peel can give you gas. However, I think that you lose some of the taste without the skin, so if you don't have a problem with it, do not peel the cucumber.

Alternatives

Instead of 2 oz / 6 cl vodka, try using 1 oz / 3 cl vodka and 1 oz / 3 cl Zubrowka for a more herbal version.

Cucumber Martini #2

Ingredients

2 oz gin

½ oz / 1½ cl sugar syrup

2½ inch / 6 cm chopped
   cucumber

Preparation

• Muddle the cucumber in the
base of the shaker.

• Add the rest of the ingredients
and shake with ice.

• Double strain into a chilled glass.

• Garnish with a cucumber spiral,
or a long slice of cucumber.

Recommendations

I strongly recommend Hendrick's Gin, which is infused with cucumber and rose petals.

=== **Variations** ===

**This drink is equally good, some
might say even better, with gin.**

Apple Martini

Glass

Cocktail

When made well this may be the best of the Fruit Martinis, with the natural sourness of apples preventing the cocktail from being too sweet. Apples and their juices vary widely in taste and sweetness. A muddled apple will not yield a large amount of juice, so I suggest you supplement with freshly pressed juice. There are three recipes below, to cover (nearly) all eventualities. Consistency is everything: know your ingredients!

Apple Martini #1

Ingredients

2 oz / 6 cl vodka

½ oz / 1½ cl apple schnapps, or apple liqueur

1 oz / 3 cl freshly pressed apple juice

½ green apple

1 dash of sugar syrup

Preparation

• Muddle the apple in the base of the shaker.

• Add the rest of the ingredients and shake with ice.

• Double strain into a chilled glass.

• Garnish with an apple slice.

Tips

• Timing is important when making this drink. Apple flesh turns brown rather rapidly, so once you've chopped your fruit and sliced the garnish you need to move quickly.

• Freshly pressed apple juice can vary in taste, so check carefully before adding sugar syrup.

Recommendations

• A piece of muddled fresh ginger can add a spicy kick.

• Try using Zubrowka instead of regular vodka. Zubrowka and apple are made for each other, and together produce a kind of nutty, Earl Grey tea quality that is simply incredible.

Apple Martini #2 (simple)

Ingredients

2 oz / 6 cl vodka

2 oz / 6 cl freshly pressed apple juice

½ oz / 1½ cl sugar syrup

Preparation

• Shake ingredients with ice.

• Double strain into a chilled glass.

• Garnish with an apple slice.

Apple Martini #3

Ingredients

1½ oz / 4½ cl vodka

1 oz / 3 cl apple schnapps, or apple liqueur

2 oz / 6 cl freshly pressed apple juice

1 dash sugar syrup

Preparation

• Shake ingredients together.

• Double strain into a chilled glass.

• Garnish with apple slice.

Tip

I prefer Apple schnapps brands without the artificial green color.

Apple Martini

Vanilla Lychee Martini

Vanilla Lychee Martini

Glass
Cocktail

This one is for those with a slightly sweeter tooth. Lychees are almost creamy in texture when muddled and shaken. Use vanilla vodka rather than regular vodka. I would serve this as a dessert drink after an Asian style meal. Despite its sweetness, it is very refreshing.

This is one occasion where I would advocate the use of canned fruit over natural. Fresh lychees are difficult to work with, and they have a peculiar after taste if they're not exactly ripe. Furthermore, the juice in the can makes a great ingredient. By all means, use real lychees for garnish if you can, as they're far more attractive than canned lychees!

Ingredients

2 oz / 6 cl vanilla flavored or
   infused vodka
1 oz / 3 cl canned lychee juice
½ oz / 1½ cl sugar syrup
3 – 4 canned lychees

Preparation

• Muddle the lychees in the base of the shaker.
• Add the rest of the ingredients and shake with ice.
• Double strain into a chilled glass.
• Garnish with lychee.

Recommendations

• Substitute vanilla syrup or even lychee syrup for the sugar syrup, to boost flavor.
• I like to serve this drink with vanilla sugar around the rim of the glass.

Optional

• If you can find a decent brand of lychee liqueur, add ½ oz / 1½ cl to give the lychee an extra kick.
• If you want to add an extra exotic twist to this drink, add a splash of rosewater and float a white rose petal on the surface of the finished cocktail. Beware – rosewater can sometimes be over-bearing and not to everyone's palate, so use sparingly.

Watermelon
& Basil Martini

Glass
Cocktail

Another strange combination at first glance, but keep an open mind. These two ingredients go very well together. Watermelon is an excellent source of nutrition, high in Vitamins A, C, B1 and B6, as well as antioxidants, magnesium and potassium. It is made up of more than 90% water, making it a great source of rehydration, fat free and filling at the same time. And if that wasn't enough, it can apparently reduce the severity of asthma, and help reduce the risk of prostate and colon cancers, heart disease, and arthritis. Having said all that, you should remember that I'm a bartender, and therefore probably the last person you should ever take medical advice from!

Ingredients

2 oz / 6 cl vodka

2–2½ oz / 6–7½ cl watermelon purée*

½ oz / 1½ cl sugar syrup

5 basil leaves, torn

Preparation

• Combine all the ingredients and shake with ice.

• Double strain into a chilled glass.

• Garnish with a leaf of basil floating on the surface.

Tips

* I usually purée my watermelon: Cut the skin away from the flesh and discard (or use for pickling or cooking). Place the flesh in a blender until you have a nice smooth purée.

• Watermelons can be rather large and cumbersome, and to cut one up for a couple of drinks might not seem worth the effort. I quite often make a batch of purée and freeze it in ice cube trays, so that I can take out as much as I need at any time.

Choosing a watermelon

• It's essential that your watermelon is ripe. Unripe watermelon is utterly bland, and you'll have a very disappointing drink.

• Choosing a ripe watermelon can be tricky. Everyone has their own method, but some of the most basic are:

Weight – a ripe fruit will be heavier than an unripe one of the same size.

Density – tap or thump a few fruits to check for a low, hollow note.

Yellow spot – look for the spot near the top of the watermelon, where the fruit lay on the ground. It should be more yellow than white (white = unripe).

Alternatives

• Ginger is also great with watermelon, although you might want to leave out the basil, or the drink might feel a bit crowded.

Options

• Here are some other flavors for you to experiment with: Strawberry / Strawberry and Balsamic Vinegar / Raspberry / Apple and Blackberry / Apple and Elderflower / Kiwi / Pineapple / Pineapple and Cardamom / Mango / Pomegranate / Carrot, Orange and Ginger.

• Try to pick stronger flavors – for example, as much as I love eating plums, I have never been happy with my attempts at a Plum Martini, as the taste of the fruit tends to get lost.

• Don't be afraid to mix in herbs and spices as the mood takes you. I repeat – there are no mistakes! It's only a drink, and if it doesn't work just pour it out and try again.

• In fact, you can make a whole cocktail party based on this premise. Buy a whole variety of ingredients and encourage your guests to use their imagination (you can even pull ingredient names out of a hat!). Even if the results are dreadful, it will only get more interesting — and funnier — as the evening wears on.

Chocolate Martini

Glass
Cocktail

Ingredients

2 oz / 6 cl vodka

2 oz / 6 cl Crème de Cacao White (Blanc)

Dash of sugar syrup (optional)

Preparation

• Shake the ingredients with ice.

• Double strain into a chilled glass with chocolate around the rim.*

Tips

• Don't be tempted to shake real chocolate into your cocktail – it doesn't work.

* To decorate the glass, pour a dash of Crème de cacao onto a plate and, holding the glass upside down, carefully wet the rim. Then gently dip it into another plate of your favorite grated chocolate and shake off the excess.

• The optional dash of sugar syrup entirely depends on you, your palate, and which brands you're using.

Chocolate & Hazelnut Martini

Just a small addition makes a big difference, and gives the cocktail a whole new dynamic.

Ingredients

2 oz / 6 cl vodka

1½ oz / 4½ cl Crème de Cacao White (Blanc)

½ oz / 1½ cl Frangelico, or hazelnut liqueur

Dash of sugar syrup (optional)

Preparation

• Shake all the ingredients with ice.

• Double strain into a chilled glass with chocolate around the rim.

Mint Chocolate Martini

A very nice after-dinner cocktail indeed.

Ingredients

2 oz / 6 cl vodka

1½ oz / 4½ cl Crème de Cacao White (Blanc)

½ oz / 1½ cl Crème de menthe white (blanc)

Dash of sugar syrup (optional)

Preparation

• Shake all the ingredients with ice.

• Double strain into a chilled glass with chocolate around the rim.

Chili Chocolate Martini

Ingredients

2 oz / 6 cl pepper or chili vodka

1½ oz / 4½ cl Crème de Cacao White (Blanc)

½ oz / 1½ cl Frangelico, or hazelnut liqueur

6 drops of Tabasco Pepper Sauce

Dash of sugar syrup

½ oz / 1½ cl heavy cream (optional)**

** While the cream is optional, I find it helps to bind all the ingredients and disparate tastes, so they slip down smoothly, rather than charge at you running and shouting!

Preparation

• Shake all the ingredients with ice.

• Double strain into a chilled glass with chocolate around the rim.

Moscow Mule

Glass

Collins (or a Moscow Mule Copper Mug, of course...)

Back in 1941, John G. Martin of G.F. Hueblein Brothers, Inc., met up with John "Jack" Morgan, owner of the famous Hollywood Cock 'n' Bull Saloon, in Chatam's Bar, New York. Martin had just acquired the rights to Smirnoff Vodka, and was wondering how to sell this little known spirit to a gin-loving America, and Morgan was having trouble shifting his own brand of ginger beer that he had just launched. The result was one of the most popular drinks of the 40's and 50's. The drink was originally served in specially designed Moscow Mule copper mugs as part of the marketing campaign.

Ingredients

2 oz / 6 cl vodka

½ oz / 1½ cl freshly squeezed
    lime juice

2 dashes of Angostura Bitters

Top off with ginger beer

Preparation

• Build the ingredients in the glass
over ice.

• Garnish with a wedge of lime.

Tips

Don't mistake ginger beer for
ginger ale – you need the spice of
ginger beer for this drink.

Recommendations

I like to squeeze 3 or 4 lime
wedges into a Moscow Mule
instead of using just juice.
Somehow it gives the drink even
more character.

════════ **Variations** ════════

Jamaican Mule – substitute
spiced rum for the vodka
French Mule – substitute
cognac for the vodka

═══════════════════════

Raspberry Mule

A really nice, fruity twist on
the classic recipe

Ingredients

10–12 raspberries

2 oz / 6 cl vodka

½ oz / 1½ cl freshly squeezed
    lime juice

2 dashes of Angostura Bitters
    (optional)

Top off with ginger beer

Preparation

• Muddle raspberries in the base
of a shaker.

• Add the next three ingredients
and shake with ice.

• Strain into a glass with ice.

• Top off with ginger beer.

• Garnish with raspberries and
a sprig of mint.

Tip

You may want to add a dash of
sugar syrup, depending on the
sourness of the raspberries.

Harvey Wallbanger

Glass
Collins

The stories about the birth of this drink nearly all involve a Manhattan Beach (CA) surfer called Harvey, who, after drinking one too many of this concoction, the way home for him and his surfboard was suddenly strewn with all manner of unavoidable obstacles, such as walls and furniture... The nickname "Wallbanger" stuck, both to him, and his new drink.

Ingredients

2 oz / 6 cl vodka

4 oz / 12 cl freshly squeezed orange juice

½ oz / 1½ cl Galliano

Preparation

• Build the vodka and freshly squeezed orange juice together on ice.

• Float the Galliano on top of the drink.

• Garnish with a slice of orange.

Tips

This is a great example of how a simple drink of two ingredients, like a Screwdriver, can be transformed by a small addition. There's orange juice, and then there's freshly squeezed orange juice. The difference is huge!

═══ **Variations** ═══

If you substitute gold tequila for the vodka, you make a Freddy Fudpucker. **Only drink this cocktail for as long as you can say it...**

Long Island Iced Tea

Glass
Collins

The ultimate Happy Hour cocktail? A drink that everyone should try once, perhaps as an ice breaker – or even just for the sake of nostalgia. Long Island Iced Tea is believed to have come from the Oak Beach Inn, Long Island in the 1970's.

Ingredients

½ oz / 1½ cl vodka

½ oz / 1½ cl white rum

½ oz / 1½ cl gin

½ oz / 1½ cl tequila

½ oz / 1½ cl Triple Sec

1 oz / 3 cl freshly squeezed lime juice

Top off with cola

Preparation

• Shake the first six ingredients with ice.

• Strain into a glass with ice.

• Top off with cola.

• Garnish with a wedge of lime.

Tips

• This is surprisingly easy to drink, but it has a lot of lot of different spirits – beware.

• Try not to add too much cola, so as to retain the bite of the lime.

Optional

With the same ingredients:

• Fill the glass with ice and add 2 – 3 oz / 6 – 9 cl cola.

• Shake the rest of the ingredients with ice.

• Carefully strain the contents of the shaker over the ice, to create a layered effect.

Sex on the Beach

Glass

Collins

This infamous 80's cocktail is still surprisingly popular today. Perhaps its attraction lies in the fact that, although quite a potent drink, its length and fruitiness make it go down easily. There are many different recipes, although most fall into two distinct categories.

Sex on the Beach #1

As classified by the International Bartenders Association

Ingredients

2 oz / 6 cl vodka

1 oz / 3 cl peach schnapps

2 oz / 6 cl freshly squeezed orange juice

2 oz / 6 cl cranberry juice

Preparation

• Shake all the ingredients with ice.

• Strain into a glass with ice.

• Garnish with a slice of orange.

Sex on the Beach #2

(as found in Mr Boston's Official Bartender's Guide, and popularized by TGI Fridays)

Ingredients

2 oz / 6 cl vodka

1 oz / 3 cl Midori or melon schnapps

½ oz / 1½ cl Chambord

2 oz / 6 cl freshly pressed pineapple juice

2 oz / 6 cl cranberry juice

Preparation

• Shake all the ingredients with ice.

• Strain into a glass with ice.

• Garnish with a slice of orange and a cocktail cherry.

Optional

• Both versions can be scaled down and served as Shooters – or make one drink as above and serve in several shot glasses.

• Some recipes substitute orange juice for pineapple or even use both together.

• Sometimes grenadine is used when cranberry juice is not available.

• Some recipes use coconut rum, such as Malibu, instead of vodka.

Variations

Woo Woo – Recipe #1 without the orange juice. You may want to add more cranberry juice.

Key West Cooler – Recipe #1 with coconut rum, such as Malibu, instead of peach schnapps.

Aviation

 Glass
Cocktail

This gorgeously elegant drink is subtle and complex. The recipe was supposedly created by Hugo Ensslin and appeared in his 1917 Recipes for Mixed Drinks. In 1930, Harry Craddock's seminal tome Savoy Cocktail Book repeated the recipe without one of the key ingredients. Below are the two recipes, one of which has the rather obscure key ingredient.

Recipe #1 (Ensslin)

Ingredients

2 oz / 6 cl gin
½ oz / 1½ cl freshly squeezed
    lemon juice
1 bar spoon Maraschino liqueur
1 bar spoon Crème de Violette

Preparation

• Shake all the ingredients together.
• Double strain into a chilled glass.
• Garnish with either cocktail cherry or lemon twist.

Optional

There are as many alternative recipes as there are makers of this drink. Whether the difference is a splash, a dash or a teaspoon, let your palate decide. The same goes for the recipe below.

Tips

I can't tell you whether to spend your money on a seldom used ingredient such as Crème de Violette. It adds a floral touch to a drink, and a dreamy, sky-blue haze, which perhaps gives the drink its name. Perhaps try the cocktail without first, as below, and if you love it, then consider investing.

Recipe #2 (Craddock)

Ingredients

2 oz / 6 cl gin
½ oz freshly squeezed lemon
    juice
1 bar spoon Maraschino liqueur

Preparation

• Shake all the ingredients with ice.
• Double strain into a chilled glass.
• Garnish with a cocktail cherry or lemon twist.

Tips

• This is one of those drinks that can use a little bit of an extra shake to dilute it.
• The amount of Maraschino you add is in your hands, but I recommend you take it easy.
• Again – balance is key. The relationship between the sour lemon and the sweet Maraschino and Crème de Violette will make or break this drink. So start with less – you can always add more, but you can't take away.
• Don't be tempted to use the Maraschino syrup from a jar of cocktail cherries. It works in some drinks, but not this one.

Bee's Knees

Glass
Cocktail

This is a Prohibition cocktail, and the honey was either meant to disguise the smell of the illegal liqueur, or hide the taste of the harsh bathtub gin. It only appeared in print, however, in David Embury's 1948 The Fine Art of Mixing Drinks. There is some debate whether orange juice should be added or not, and indeed Embury does not.

Ingredients
2 oz / 6 cl gin
1 oz / 3 cl freshly squeezed
   lemon juice
1 oz / 3 cl freshly squeezed
   orange juice
½ oz / 1½ cl or 3 bar spoons
   runny honey

Preparation
• Add the honey and gin to the shaker and stir until the honey dissolves.
• Add the rest of the ingredients and shake with ice.
• Double strain into a chilled glass.
• Garnish with a twist of lemon.

Optional
Leave out the orange juice, and knock the lemon juice down to ½ oz / 1½ cl.

Bramble

Glass
Rocks

Another contemporary classic from Dick Bradsell, which is so astoundingly simple, it's hard to believe that no one thought of it before! If you get the balance right, you should be able to feel each component of the drink at work as it rolls over your tongue, and how it contributes to the final taste.

Ingredients
2 oz / 6 cl gin
1 oz / 3 cl freshly squeezed
   lemon juice
½ oz / 1½ cl sugar syrup
½ oz / 1½ cl Crème de Mure

Preparation
• Shake the first three ingredients with ice.
• Strain into a glass with crushed ice.
• Float Crème de Mure on the top of the drink.
• Garnish with lemon and (if available) blackberries.

Recommendations
I like to add a sprig of fresh mint to the garnish, both for color and aroma. Would a touch of fresh ginger be overdoing it?

Tip
It's tempting to overdo it with the Crème de Mure – as always, start with less, you can always add more.

Dry Martini

And so we come to what is, perhaps, the most talked about cocktail of them all. The drink of Nixon, J.F.K., George Bush Senior, Churchill, F. Scott Fitzgerald, Dorothy Parker, Carey Grant, Humphrey Bogart, Dean Martin, Noel Coward, W.C. Fields, Ernest Hemingway (well, one of his...), among many, many others. Stories of the invention of the Martini range from the early 19th Century up to 1911. Most cocktail historians agree that a drink called the Martinez is probably the forerunner of the Martini. The Martinez itself is possibly a variation of the Manhattan; it is listed in Professor Jerry Thomas' Bartender's Guide of 1862. Towards the end of the 19th Century, London Dry gin was starting to be popular in the US, and this is the first crucial switch – although it's hard to pin down when. The other big change was in the vermouth.

There are a hundred ways to make a Martini. This is my way. I recommend that you try it, and then adapt it. Do whatever you want with a Martini. I have followed the recipe with just some of the myriad of variations that exist. In the meantime, just decide – olive or a twist?

(continued on page 56)

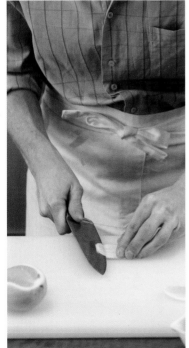

Dry Martini

(continued from page 54)

 Glass
Cocktail (Martini!)

Ingredients

2 oz / 6 cl your favorite brand of gin
A liberal slug of dry vermouth

Preparation

• Fill a mixing glass or glass part of the shaker full with fresh ice.
• Add the vermouth.
• Swirl the shaker around for 10 – 15 seconds, making sure the vermouth coats all the ice.
• Strain off all the vermouth – leaving you with vermouth coated ice.
• Add the gin to the mixing glass or shaker.
• Stir 52 times (you can change direction every 10 stirs).
• Double strain into a chilled glass.

Garnish

Either

Olive – your choice as to type and how many, as long as it's green.

Or

Spray the oil from a lemon twist over the drink, wipe the twist around the rim of the glass, and drop it inside.

Tips

• The long stirring is because an essential part of a Martini is water, which comes from the ice. Your drink will end up being between ¼ – ⅓ water.
• It's absolutely imperative that you make this cocktail with your favorite brand, whatever that may be, otherwise it's pointless...!
• Bigger is often more beautiful when it comes to cocktail glasses. But don't be tempted to super-size your drink to fit the glass. A Martini should be drunk ice cold and quick, not slow and warm.

Recommendations

• Many old recipes call for a couple of drops of orange bitters, and I fully recommend this.
• If someone asks you to make them a Martini relish the challenge. Ask what brand (if you have options), and whether they prefer an olive or a twist.
• Refer to Variations below if these questions are not enough.

=== **Variations** ===
Roosevelt – **garnished with 2 olives.**
Gibson – **garnished with 2 small pearl onions.**
Dickens – **no garnish.**

Shaken or Stirred?

• Modern style dictates that a Martini is stirred.
• Shaking 'bruises the gin', which adds minuscule bubbles to the drink, making it cloudy; it leaves small shards of ice floating on the top of the drink; it also mixes oxygen with the aldehyde molecules within liqueur, altering the taste slightly.
• A shaken Martini is correctly called a **Bradford**.
• Ah 007... Never one to do things the traditional way. Perhaps a man of action who liked the idea of bruising something? Or did he know that shaking a Martini increases its antioxidant effect? Or was he just wiser than we think? Vodka, especially when made from potatoes, can be oily, and shaking disperses the oil more than stirring.

Glass
Cocktail (or Champagne Saucer)

Vodka Martini

Some people swear by a vodka Martini, but as a professed gin fan, I find it hard to get over-excited by a vodka Martini unless it's drunk exceptionally quickly. Substitute your favorite brand of vodka for the gin.

Dirty Martini

Make your Dry Martini as above, but add to the shaker some brine from the olive jar. The question, of course, is how much? Start with no more than a teaspoon. Then go upwards from there, according to your taste. Caution! - there is a point where you can add too much brine, and a Dirty Martini just becomes filthy...

Vesper Martini

The following is the creation of a legend, from Casino Royale, by Ian Fleming:

A dry martini," [Bond] said. "One. In a deep champagne goblet."
"Oui, monsieur."
"Just a moment. Three measures of Gordon's, one of vodka, half a measure of Kina Lillet. Shake it very well until it's ice-cold, then add a large thin slice of lemon peel. Got it?"
"Certainly, monsieur." The barman seemed pleased with the idea.
"Gosh, that's certainly a drink," said Leiter.
Bond laughed. "When I'm...er...concentrating," he explained, "I never have more than one drink before dinner. But I do like that one to be large and very strong and very cold and very well-made. I hate small portions of anything, particularly when they taste bad.
This drink's my own invention. I'm going to patent it when I can think of a good name."

The Martini, as ordered by James Bond in Casino Royale, is powerful stuff indeed, and actually rather difficult to re-create. One of the key ingredients is Kina Lillet, now known simply as Lillet Blanc, whose formula was changed in 1986, and now contains less quinine, making the drink less bitter. Furthermore you should really use a 100% proof grain vodka.

Ingredients
3 oz / 9 cl gin
1 oz / 3 cl vodka
½ oz / 1½ cl dry vermouth – preferably Lillet Blanc (would you argue with 007?)

Preparation
• Shake the ingredients with ice.
• Double strain into a chilled glass.
• Garnish with a strip of lemon.

Gimlet

Glass
Cocktail

Did you ever wonder why Americans call Englishmen 'Limeys?' This cocktail holds the answer... In 1867 A Scottish shipyard owner began producing Rose's Lime Cordial without alcohol. The British Navy had long known that citrus fruit helped keep the scurvy at bay but had no way of keeping the necessary amount of fresh fruit on board for long periods of time. This new product provided the solution. Rose's Lime Cordial was so successful that British sailors soon became known as 'Limeys' across the Caribbean and the Americas.

Ingredients
2 oz / 6 cl gin
1 oz / 3 cl Rose's Lime Cordial

Preparation
• Shake the ingredients with ice.
• Double strain into a chilled glass.
• Garnish with a wedge of lime.

Tip
This is the only use I can think of for Lime Cordial. Some bartenders use it in other drinks, but I prefer fresh lime and sugar.

Options
Charles Schumann, author of the most excellent 'American Bar,' advocates adding fresh lime juice. Squeeze a couple of lime wedges into the shaker and add the husks when shaking, to get all the oil out of the skin.

=== **Variations** ===

Vodka Gimlet
substitute vodka for the gin

Martinez

Glass
Cocktail

No one knows for sure where the Martinez came from, but Jerry Thomas is one of the possible creators. Supposedly, he created the drink for a prospector who was about to journey to the mines of Martinez in California. However, the inhabitants of Martinez claim it was the other way around, and the local bartender, Julio Richelieu, created the drink in 1874 for our prospector on his way back to San Francisco.

Ingredients
1½ oz / 4½ cl Old Tom gin
1½ oz / 4½ cl sweet vermouth
1 dash Maraschino liqueur
1 dash Angostura Bitters

Preparation
• Stir all the ingredients in a mixing glass.
• Double strain into a chilled glass.
• Spray the oil from a twist of orange over the drink, wipe it around the rim of the glass and drop it inside.

Monkey Gland

Glass
Cocktail

The name was given by its creator Harry MacElhone, of Harry's New York Bar, Paris, in the 1920's, and was inspired by the work of Dr. Serge Voronoff, who was famous for conducting experiments to reduce the aging process in males by grafting monkey tissue onto his patients.Incredibly, his work was deemed very fashionable in the 1920's.

Recipe #1

Ingredients
2 oz / 6 cl gin
1 oz / 3 cl freshly squeezed
    orange juice
¼ oz / ¾ cl absinthe
¼ oz / ¾ cl grenadine

Preparation
• Shake all the ingredients with ice.
• Double strain into a chilled glass.
• Garnish with an orange twist.

Recipe #2

Ingredients
2 oz / 6 cl gin
1 oz / 3 cl freshly squeezed
    orange juice
½ oz / 1½ cl Benedictine
¼ oz / ¾ cl grenadine

Preparation
• Shake all the ingredients with ice.
• Double strain into a chilled glass.
• Garnish with an orange twist.

Ramos Gin Fizz

Glass
Collins (large)

This is an extraordinary drink, rather like the soufflé of the cocktail world. I'm warning you now, it's a bit tricky, and it requires orange flower water, which can be difficult to find. Created in 1888 by Henry C. Ramos at the bar in Meyer's Restaurant, the original recipe demands that it be shaken for 12 minutes! The key to the drink is the emulsification of the egg-white with the rest of the ingredients.

a.k.a. New Orleans Gin Fizz

Ingredients
2 oz / 6 cl gin
½ oz / 1½ cl freshly squeezed
    lemon juice
½ oz / 1½ cl freshly squeezed
    lime juice
1 oz / 3 cl sugar syrup
1 oz / 3 cl heavy cream
1 egg white
3 dashes orange flower water
Soda water (preferably from
    a siphon)

Preparation
• Shake the first seven ingredients without ice for at least one minute, but much longer is better.
• Add ice and shake for basically as long as you can – the drink must be very cold and very frothy.
• Strain into a chilled glass with no ice.
• Top with soda water and stir vigorously to froth it up.

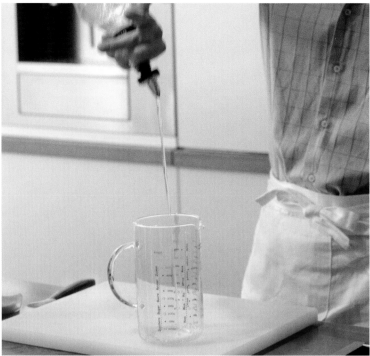

Negroni

Negroni

Glass
Cocktail

This drink is most definitely high on the short list for my favorite cocktail of all time – it's certainly the best aperitif I know. It's perfectly, but oh so perfectly balanced, complex, and strangely cleansing. The story goes that a certain Count Camillo Negroni was in his favorite bar in Florence and ordered an "Americano with a kick." This is the result, and I give thanks to the Count every time I raise a Negroni to my lips.

I hope that up to now you have found me quite laid back, and not too fussy... Well, I'm afraid with this cocktail, one of my most beloved, I have supplied no other options, and if you drink it any other way, I shall never speak to you again!

Variations

Negroni Spumante – **OK, so one variation is acceptable: Top it up with champagne. You may want to use a larger glass.**

Ingredients

1 oz / 3 cl gin
1 oz / 3 cl Campari
1 oz / 3 cl Punt e Mes vermouth*

Preparation

• Stir the ingredients 52 times in a mixing glass.
• Double strain immediately into a chilled glass.
• Spray the oil from an orange twist over the drink, wipe it around the rim of the glass and drop it in.

Recommendations

* I'm fairly liberal when it comes to brands – each to their own. But where sweet or red vermouth is concerned, it's either Punt e Mes or nothing. It may be a little harder to find, but it's absolutely worth it, and this cocktail, like a Sweet Manhattan, is just not the same without it.
• Many serve this drink on ice. I think it deserves the elegance of a cocktail glass, and furthermore, I don't like the way it can get diluted towards the end when there is ice.
• The orange twist really makes this drink!
• If you do change the recipe in some way, just please, please, don't tell me...

Singapore Sling

Glass
Collins (or Sling if you can find one)

Yet another old school classic and a damned fine drink too.
Long and fruity, yet not too sweet, with a hint of spice.
It was invented at the Raffles Hotel in Singapore by Ngiam
Tong Boom. I have tried this drink in many forms, and below
is the recipe that I like. If you enjoy it, then I suggest you try
other versions.

So what is so special about gin? It starts life as a very similar
liqueur to vodka, and is then re-distilled with juniper berries
(which provide the dominant aroma when you smell gin),
and other spices and essential oils known as botanicals.
Gin was originally distilled as a medicine (it was taken
liberally during outbreaks of bubonic plague, to absolutely
no good effect whatsoever, although the alcoholic content
might have eased the suffering...). Depending on the
brand, botanicals can include: juniper, coriander, caraway,
elderflower, chamomile, anise, angelica root, meadowsweet,
orris root, cubeb, lemon oil, orange oil, grapefruit oil,
nutmeg, cinnamon, saffron, licorice, frankincense, cassia
bark, almond, savory, and many others. The most common
style of gin nowadays is London Dry, whose production is
carefully restricted, and cannot contain any added sugar or
coloring. However, gin actually comes from Holland, and is
the original 'Dutch Courage' (it was given to Dutch soldiers
before battle to calm their nerves). Dutch or Jenever Gin is
sweeter, and noticeably different from London Dry as it is
partly distilled from barley.

Ingredients
1½ oz / 4½ cl gin
1 oz / 3 cl Cherry Heering or
    cherry brandy
1 oz / 3 cl freshly squeezed
    lemon juice
½ oz / 1½ cl sugar syrup
1½ oz / 4½ cl freshly pressed
    pineapple juice
Top off with ginger ale
½ oz / 1½ cl Benedictine

Preparation
• Shake the first five ingredients
with ice.
• Strain into a glass with
crushed ice.
• Top off with ginger ale.
• Drizzle Benedictine over the top
of the drink.
• Garnish with a pineapple leaf
and a cocktail cherry.

Recommendations
Although most definitely NOT
in the original recipe, I love
adding fresh muddled ginger to
this drink – if you're going to be
unorthodox, you might as well go
the whole way, no?

Singapore Sling

Tom Collins

Tom Collins

Glass
Collins

Where does it come from? Well as always, there are many versions. The favorites are that a bartender called John Collins, of Limmer's Hotel in London, created it, perhaps even as early as 1814. It is more likely, however, to be of American origin, and perhaps takes its name from the Great Tom Collins Hoax of 1874 (yes, you read correctly!), a contagious practical joke where the joker would enter a bar and tell his victim that a certain Tom Collins was in a bar just around the corner, bad-mouthing him (the victim). However, the first proper mention of the Tom Collins cocktail appears in the 1876 second edition of Jerry Thomas' The Bartender's Guide. What should a Tom Collins be made with? Jerry Thomas only muddies the waters further. First of all he lists recipes for brandy, whisky and gin Tom Collins. While it is generally accepted today that a Tom Collins is made with gin, he fails to mention which gin!

Today there is a very large extended family of Collins. The most well known are Tom and John, although no one can really tell them apart. In various sources, you can find both listed being made with all three types of gin. I'm going to stick my neck out, and take a stand!

Tom Collins – Old Tom
John Collins – Jenever
If you only have London Dry in the cupboard, then call it what you want, or simply a Gin Collins!

Ingredients

1½–2 oz / 4½–6 cl Old Tom gin
1 oz / 3 cl freshly squeezed
   lemon juice
1 teaspoon fine white sugar or
   ½ oz sugar syrup
Top off with soda water

Preparation

• Add the first three ingredients to the shaker and stir to dissolve the sugar.
• Shake with ice.
• Strain into a glass, add ice, and fill with soda water.
• Garnish with a slice of lemon, a slice of orange, and a cherry.
• In the immortal words of Jerry Thomas - "imbibe while it is lively".

Tip

The use of fine sugar is making a comeback with those who appreciate originality.

Optional

It goes without saying that you can substitute almost any liqueur for the Old Tom gin, and whatever you want to call it is fine by me.

Variations

There's a modern trend to soup up the Collins with fruits and liqueurs, which I whole-heartedly recommend that you try.

White Lady

Glass
Cocktail

I absolutely love making this drink. It looks fantastic, and it's a great way to introduce someone to cocktails. It's not too strong, smooth as you like, and perfectly sweet and sour. On paper it looks relatively simple, although the prospect of egg white alarms some. But if you ever need convincing of the use of egg white in cocktails, make a White Lady with and without, and I promise you'll be convinced.

Two giants of the cocktail world claim this drink. The first is Harry MacElhone, in 1923 at his Harry's New York Bar in Paris. The second is Harry Craddock, at the Savoy Bar who included it in his 1930 Savoy Cocktail Book (according to sources at the Savoy it was a favorite of Laurel and Hardy). There are some variations in the recipes, but the one I give below has served me well for many years, and I don't mess with it.

Ingredients
1½ oz / 4½ cl gin
1 oz / 3 cl Cointreau
1 oz / 3 cl freshly squeezed
   lemon juice
1 dash of sugar syrup
1 egg white

Preparation
• Shake all the ingredients
with ice.
• Double strain into a chilled glass.
• Dust with grated nutmeg.

Tips
• Many recipes don't use sugar. I find a small amount rounds this cocktail out nicely, and lifts all the different tastes. If you prefer it sour, omit the sugar syrup.
• I know I sound like a broken record, but the balance of this drink is crucial! This is why I add sugar syrup. If you don't balance the sourness of the lemon, the drink can feel a bit flat, or just rather lemony. But easy does it – it's very easy to make this drink too sweet, which is not good. Remember – start with less, and add more if necessary.
• It's not written in any recipe, but if there just happens to be some around (which is not very often!), I can't resist adding a white rose petal as a garnish. I can hear the protests of the purists, but what the heck, it looks great.

White Lady

Chelsea Sidecar – without the egg white, but with sugar syrup. Boxcar – substitute grenadine for the sugar syrup and serve in a sugar-rimmed glass. Breakfast Martini (Salvatore Calabrese's invention) – replace the sugar syrup and egg white with one bar spoon of fine sliced, good quality orange marmalade. Lady Marmalade (I believe this is my friend, Wayne Collins' twist) – replace the sugar syrup and egg white with one bar spoon of good quality apricot jam.

Rum & Tequila Cocktails

03

Rum & Tequila

Cocktails

The history of rum is intrinsically linked to the West's dependence on sugar; Rum's modern history meanders from the English Reformation of 1584, through the explorations of Columbus and Magellan, interweaving itself with the ensuing centuries of colonialism and naval history, slavery and human trafficking, smuggling, piracy and revolution. More than anything, rum is the soothing companion to the painful modern history of the Caribbean. The first rum distillery in Colonial America was built on Staten Island in 1664, and rum quickly became New England's most profitable industry. In general, rum takes on a different hue and taste, depending on its age: from silver or white through gold, to dark (beware of coloring and additives, however).

The world of tequila cocktails has been utterly dominated, for better or worse, by one drink – the Margarita, which now seems to inhabit its own universe of various quality, flavors and accessories. Tequila is now being promoted as a liqueur to be savored, and treated like a fine whisky, rum, or cognac, to be sipped from a nice glass, accompanied by a cigar. Tequila is made from the Blue Agave (also known as the Tequilana Agave Azul, Weber's Blue Agave, or to the locals, Maguey), a plant of the same genus as Yucca. It has been made since the 16th century in and around the town of Tequila, in the Western Mexican state of Jalisco.

Bahama Mama

Glass

Collins

Using this recipe as a template you can create a whole range of great summer party cocktails just by changing the juices, and / or the liqueurs. Note the use of different rums to build up layers of taste.

Ingredients

½ oz / 1½ cl dark over-proof or Navy rum

½ oz / 1½ cl dark rum

½ oz / 1½ cl coconut rum or liqueur

1½ oz / 4½ cl freshly squeezed orange juice

2 oz / 6 cl freshly pressed pineapple juice

½ oz freshly squeezed lime juice

2 dashes of Angostura Bitters

Preparation

• Shake all the ingredients with ice.

• Strain into a glass filled with crushed ice.

• Garnish with a chunk of pineapple.

Tip

Bad or cheap dark rum, especially Navy or over-proof, can be diabolical – beware. The cheaper you go, the worse your drink will taste and you will feel.

Alternatives

If so inclined, you can add a dash of Kahlua into the mix.

Bossa Nova

Glass

Collins

This is a great drink, fruity but not too sweet, very smooth, and the Galliano adds a nice touch of complexity frolicking somewhere in your mouth.

Ingredients

1½ oz / 4½ cl white rum

½ oz / 1½ cl apricot brandy

½ oz / 1½ cl Galliano

2 oz / 6 cl freshly pressed pineapple juice

½ oz freshly squeezed lemon juice

½ white of an egg

Preparation

• Shake all the ingredients.

• Strain into a glass with crushed ice.

• Garnish with a chunk of pineapple.

Alternatives

You can use freshly pressed apple juice instead of pineapple.

Caipirinha (see opposite page) really is the national cocktail of Brazil. The word 'Caipira' means 'hick,' or 'hill-billy,' so you're actually drinking a little country bumpkin! Cachaça is traditionally a peasant liqueur, and a liter (33.8 fl. oz.) will set you back just over $1 in Brazil, making it cheaper than bottled mineral water. Nowadays, you can buy much more refined, aged Cachaça, at much higher prices.

Caipirinha

Glass

Glass
Old Fashioned

Ingredients

1 lime
2 bar spoons of fine sugar
(to taste)
2 oz / 6 cl Cachaça

Preparation
• Cut the lime into 8 cubes.
• Muddle the lime with the sugar, in the metal part of a shaker.*
• Transfer to a glass.
• Add ice and Cachaça and stir.
• Top off with ice if necessary.

Recommendations
* I can't recommend strongly enough that you muddle your lime in the metal part of a shaker. Doing it straight in the glass is not a good idea. Believe me, from personal experience, breaking a glass while you're holding it in your hand is more than irritating, and is a waste of a good lime! And blood does not make the drink taste better.

• I like to use natural brown, or Turbinado sugar, to give a richer taste.
• I prefer to keep the lime and add extra fruit. A mixture of berries, for example, makes a fantastic drink. Take a handful of raspberries, strawberries and blackberries (and maybe even some ginger) and muddle them with the lime, and then add the ice and Cachaça.

=== **Variations** ===

Caipifrutas – almost exactly like the Batidas, you can substitute nearly any fruit you like for the lime.
Caipirovska – substitute vodka for the Cachaça
Caipirissima – substitute white rum for the Cachaça

Batidas

Glass
Collins

Batida Abacaxí (Pineapple)

Ingredients

Big chunk of fresh pineapple
(optional)*
2 oz / 6 cl Cachaça
2 oz / 6 cl freshly pressed
pineapple juice
½ oz / 1½ cl freshly squeezed
lime juice
½ oz / 1½ cl sugar syrup

Preparation
• If you're using fresh pineapple, muddle it in the base of a shaker.
• Add the rest of the ingredients and shake with ice.
• Strain into a glass with crushed ice.*

• Garnish with a chunk of pineapple.
or
• Blend all the ingredients and pour into a glass with crushed ice.*
• Garnish with a chunk of pineapple.

Tips
* Whether you add pineapple for muddling or for blending depends on you. The blender will give you a smoother, thicker drink. Just don't use canned pineapple!
• You can use condensed milk for Batidas, but if you do, omit the lime juice and sugar.

Most Cachaça (rum made from fermented sugar cane) is cheap, and pretty rough on the palate, but when mixed with fresh fruits, it can be divine. You can have a great time exploring the whole range of Batida drinks and inventing a few as you go along.

(continued on page 72)

(continued from page 71)

Glass

Collins

Batida Maracujá (Passion Fruit)

Ingredients

The pulp of 1 or 2 passion fruit
    (depending on size)
2 oz / 6 cl Cachaça
1 oz / 3 cl condensed milk
Dash sugar syrup – to taste

Preparation

• Shake all the ingredients.*

• Strain into a glass with
crushed ice.

Tips

* I would not recommend
blending, as passion fruit is filled
with seeds.

• If you can find good, fresh
passion fruit juice, you may want
to lengthen the cocktail.

• Passion fruit is acidic, so you
may want to add sugar to taste,
but try not to spoil the natural
sourness.

Batida de Milho Verde (Sweet Corn)

No really, I'm serious!
Try it once – it's amazing...

Ingredients

2 oz / 6 cl Cachaça
2 oz / 6 cl condensed milk
2 tablespoons of sweet corn

Preparation

• Blend all the ingredients
until smooth.

• Pour into a glass with
crushed ice.

=== **Variations** ===

Batida Morango **(strawberry) –
you can add Crème de Fraises to
boost the taste.**
Batida Carneval
(mango) – blend this one.
Batida Banana
Pineapple and Sweet Pepper –
**blend, and throw in some chili
pepper if you like.**

Batida de Coco (Coconut)

Ingredients

2 oz / 6cl Cachaça
2 oz / 6cl coconut cream
1 oz / 3cl condensed milk

Preparation

• Shake all the ingredients.

• Strain into a glass with
crushed ice.

Batida de Liete Onça (Jaguar's Milk)

Ingredients

2 oz / 6 cl Cachaça
2 oz / 6 cl condensed milk
1 oz / 3 cl Crème de Cacao brown

Preperation

• Shake all the ingredients.

• Strain into a glass with
crushed ice.

• Sprinkle nutmeg, cinnamon,
or grated chocolate on top.

There are no rules when it comes to Batidas, so – anything goes! They
are basically Cachaça with fruit or fruit juice, sweetened with sugar,
or with 'liete condensado,' (condensed milk), if you want a creamy,
milkshake style drink. While not exactly traditional, many people now
use a blender to make their Batidas, particularly if using fresh fruits.

Harder to find ingredients

Batida de Cupuaçu
you'll have to look hard,
but many claim Cupuaçu
is the new superfruit.
Batida de Graviola
(Soursop / Guanabana) –
check in Latino stores.
Batida de Caju
(Cashew Fruit – not the nut).

Tips
• When you experiment,
decide whether you want the
creaminess of the condensed
milk, and how smooth you want
your finished drink to be, i.e. to
blend or not to blend.
• Don't be afraid to add a dash of
freshly squeezed lime juice into
the mix for a sharper taste.

Batida Maracujá

Red Grapefruit
& Basil Caipirinha

Glass
Old Fashioned

I would love to say I invented this, but I'm sure someone out there beat me to it....

Ingredients

¼ red grapefruit

2 bar spoons of fine sugar

1 oz / 3 cl freshly pressed red grapefruit juice

2 oz / 6 cl Cachaça

½ oz / 1½ cl Campari *

5 – 6 basil leaves **

Preparation

• Cut the red grapefruit into cubes.

• Muddle with sugar in the metal part of a shaker.

• Add the rest of the ingredients and shake with crushed ice.

• Pour the contents of the shaker into a glass.

• Garnish with a red grapefruit wedge and a basil leaf.

Tips

* The Campari helps the grapefruit – but if you're not a Campari fan, leave it out.

** Aesthetically, red basil is more pleasing to the eye, and it is a bit spicier, but it's not essential.

Cubed or crushed ice? It's up to the drinker to stir it to the right coolness, and till the sugar is dissolved. The Brazilian method is usually to use ice cubes, as opposed to the crushed ice you're probably familiar with. The drinker should stir to cool the drink down and help the sugar to dissolve. Crushed ice will make your drink cooler much quicker.

Daiquiri

Glass

Cocktail (Straight Up / "Naturel") or Collins (with ice)

The Daiquiri is an intensely simple cocktail, which perhaps makes it more difficult to get right. With long fruity drinks, quite often a splash too much here or there can go unnoticed; drinks such as the Daiquiri – not to mention the Dry Martini, Old Fashioned or Manhattan – require concentration, a steady hand and a keen eye. I suggest that, as always, you experiment and find what suits you best, but remember that the rum is the star, and too much lime or sugar will destroy the drink. And again, the quality of your ingredients is also of the utmost importance. If you're going to use a cheap rum, then I wouldn't even bother making a Daiquiri. To complicate matters there are an endless variety of Daiquiris, and that is even before we get to the fruit ones. While most variations of Dry Martinis tend to revolve around ratios, the diversity of Daiquiris is vast and subtle. There's no way that we can travel together through the Daiquiri world. I'll try and give you the basics, and after that you're on your own!

Ingredients

2 oz / 6 cl white rum

½ oz / 1½ cl freshly squeezed
   lime juice

¼ oz / ¾ cl sugar syrup

Preparation

• Shake all the ingredients
with ice.

• Double strain into a chilled
Cocktail Glass or a Collins with
cubed ice.

• Garnish with a wedge of lime.

Recommendations

• As well as trying different rums,
you could also try using,
for example, vanilla infused rum
to give your Daiquiri
a sumptuous twist.

• Try using honey instead
of sugar.

Alternatives

• Simon Difford, the ultimate
Daiquiri nerd (and I mean this
with the utmost respect – his
work is professorial) uses the ratio
of 10:3:2 for his "Naturel" Daiquiri.

• El Floridita has a published ratio
of 8:4:1, which to my mind is too
much lime.

• The International Bartenders
Association ratio is 9:4:1 –
just in case you were interested.

Tips

• I know I keep going on about
ratios, but it is important! The
classic ratio of a Daiquiri is 8:2:1
(rum: lime: sugar), as quantified
by the master and huge Daiquiri
fan, David Embury. It can be a
pain to measure ¼ oz /
¾ cl of anything, but if you stick
to the ratio you can use any
measurement you like, and get
the same result.

• Just remember that different
rums have different levels of
sweetness, so you may want to
adjust the sugar accordingly.
A Rhum Agricole works very well,
but is naturally sweeter, as are
gold rums – so beware.

• It would appear from various
sources that the drink was in fact
originally built in the glass over
ice. It was only later that it was
shaken (and then with crushed
ice – I recommend a good hard
shake with cubed ice).

Fruit Daiquiris

Glass

Cocktail

The creation of the Daiquiri is credited to an American engineer, Jennings Cox, who was exploring the iron-ore mines in the area of the town of Daiquirí, near Santiago de Cuba, around 1900. Legend has it that a fellow engineer called Pagliuchi came to meet Cox, and the host rustled up a concoction of the ingredients he had to hand, Bacardi (which was part of his food ration), lemons and sugar. It's a well documented story.

When made properly, a good fruit Daiquiri can be very pleasant. Just don't use anything artificial! No packets, no pre-mixes, no bottles of Daiquiri mix etc.

When making Fruit Daiquiris, remember you're still making a Daiquiri, and the fruit should merely compliment the rum, not overpower it. Also, a Fruit Daiquiri doesn't have to be frozen. Following is a recipe for a Daiquiri de Fresa (strawberry), but you can adapt it to other kinds of fruit. You can boost the fruit flavor by using fruit liqueurs, but try to keep it as natural as possible.

Recipe #1

Ingredients

2 oz / 6 cl white rum

½ oz / 1½ cl freshly squeezed lime juice

¼ oz / ¾ cl sugar syrup

6 or so ripe strawberries

Preparation

• Muddle the strawberries in the base of a shaker.

• Add the other ingredients and shake with ice.

• Double strain into a chilled glass.

• Garnish with a strawberry.

Recipe #2

Ingredients

2 oz / 6 cl rum

¾ oz / 2¼ cl freshly squeezed lime juice

¾ oz / 2¼ cl sugar syrup

6 or so ripe strawberries

Preparation

• Place all the ingredients on a blender with crushed ice and blend until smooth.

• Pour contents into a chilled glass.

• Garnish with a strawberry.

Fruit Daiquiris

Frozen Daiquiri

 Glass
Cocktail

 Glass
Cocktail

 Glass
Large Cocktail

Glass
Cocktail

Ingredients

2 oz / 6 cl rum

¾ oz / 2¼ cl freshly squeezed
  lime juice

¾ oz / 2¼ cl sugar syrup

1 small teaspoon of Maraschino
  liqueur

Preparation

• Place all the ingredients in
a blender with crushed ice and
blend until smooth.

• Double strain into a chilled glass.

Tip

I've adopted Simon Difford's ratio
of 8:3:3, because it's how I like it,
but check for yourself. Just don't
be tempted to use too much ice,
or you will lose all the taste.

Daiquiri #1
Papa Doble

Hemingway was averse to
sugar. He was diagnosed
with diabetes, and in 1961
(the year he took his own
life) with hemochromatosis,
so he drank his Daiquiris
very sour, with no sugar, and
being the prodigious drinker
he was, with double the
rum. The Papa Doble was
basically rum and lime, and a
very tough drink at that.

Daiquiri #2
Hemingway Daiquiri

Served

Shaken or frozen / blended

Ingredients

4 oz / 12 cl rum

1½ oz / 4½ cl freshly squeezed
  lime juice

½ oz / 1½ cl freshly squeezed
  grapefruit juice (red / pink is
  best)

½ oz / 1½ cl Maraschino liqueur

Preparation

• Place all the ingredients in
a blender with crushed ice and
blend until smooth.

• Double strain into a chilled glass.

Daiquiri #3
a.k.a. Floridita

Served

Shaken or frozen / blended

Ingredients

2 oz / 6 cl rum

½ oz / 1½ cl freshly squeezed
  lime juice

¼ oz / ¾ cl sugar syrup

½ oz / 1½ cl freshly squeezed
  grapefruit juice (red / pink
  is best)

1 small teaspoon of Maraschino
  liqueur

Preparation

• Place all the ingredients in
a blender with crushed ice and
blend until smooth.

• Double strain into a chilled glass.

Hot Buttered Rum

Glass
Toddy, or Mug

This old cocktail is one for a winter's evening, sitting by a fire. It's been around longer than the U.S.A., and I believe that if something has lasted that long, it must be for a good reason.

Ingredients

1–2 oz / 3–6 cl gold rum
(depending how cold you are...)
1 bar spoon of sugar or honey *
1 pat of butter ("as large as half a chestnut")
A few cloves wedged into a slice of lemon
2 or 3 whole allspice berries
Boiling water

Preparation

• Add all the ingredients and stir until the honey and butter are dissolved.
• Sprinkle grated nutmeg on the top of the drink.

Tips

* The original recipe uses sugar, but this drink cries out for honey.
• Experiment with your own favorite spices –cardamom or ginger for example.

Dark 'n' Stormy

Glass
Collins

This superbly deep, spicy, refreshing cocktail is really a Mule, but it's so fine that it deserves to stand alone. While rum and ginger beer are quintessentially Caribbean, the Dark 'n' Stormy is actually considered to be the national drink of Bermuda, where it is made with the local dark rum, Gosling's. It is also a hugely popular drink in Australia, where it is thought to have been introduced via the rugby Classic Tournament held in Bermuda. In Australia it is usually made with Bundaberg Rum, and, of course, Bundaberg Ginger Beer. Whatever the brand name, this is a great way to enjoy dark rum.

Ingredients

2 oz / 6 cl dark rum
1 oz / 3 cl freshly squeezed lime juice
Top off with ginger beer

Preparation

• Build the ingredients in a glass with ice and stir.
• Garnish with a wedge of lime.

Tips

• Some leave out the lime, which I personally consider almost a sin.
• Ginger beers can vary greatly, particularly those not mass-produced, so check it first, and decide if you want to add a touch of sugar syrup.
• Mules often have a dash of Angostura Bitters – this one is tough enough to go without.

Fish House Punch

Glass

Collins

Recipe – 1 serving

Ingredients

1 teaspoon superfine sugar

1 oz / 3 cl freshly squeezed
    lemon juice

1 oz / 3 cl Jamaica rum
    (such as Myers's)

1 oz / 3 cl brandy (doesn't have to
    be cognac)

½ oz / 1½ cl peach brandy

Water or soda water

Preparation

Either

• Stir the sugar with the lemon
juice in the glass.

• Add the liqueurs and ice.

• Top off with 2 oz / 6 cl mineral
water or soda water.

Or

• Shake all the ingredients, except
the water, with ice.

• Strain into a glass with ice.

• Top off with 2 oz / 6 cl mineral
water or soda water, as preferred.

Optional

Some like to top off with cold
black tea instead of water.
Nice idea.

Recipe – Batch

Receptacles

Punch bowl and punch glasses

Ingredients

2 Bottles of Jamaica rum
    (such as Myers's)

1 bottle of cognac

1 quart (4 cups) freshly squeezed
    lemon juice

1 pound of superfine sugar

8 oz / 24 cl peach brandy

Water *

Preparation

• Dissolve the sugar in the lemon
juice and some water.

• Add the rest of the ingredients.

Either

* Add 2 quarts of water and a
block of ice, as big as possible
(freeze water in a mixing bowl if
you must).

• Leave for an hour, stirring
frequently, and taste.

Or

• Add a block of ice made from
3 quarts of water.

• Leave the ice to melt, regularly
ladle the punch over the ice,
and taste.

• Refrigerate if not served
immediately.

• Serve with sliced fruit - optional.

1732 saw the founding of the Schuylkill Fishing Company of Pennsylvania, later known as the State in Schuylkill, and more informally as the Fish House. They have a legendary Punch which was first created in 1732 or 1848. If the former, it may well be the oldest punch in the English speaking world.

"There's a little place just out of town / Where, if you go to lunch / They'll make you forget your mother-in-law / With a drink called Fish-House Punch."

(From "The Cook" 1885)

Mai Tai

Glass
Old Fashioned

Another cocktail, another argument... So who created this Tiki classic? One evening, in 1944, in his restaurant in Oakland, CA, Victor Jules Beregon mixed a new drink for two friends visiting from Tahiti, Ham and Carrie Guild. Carrie was so impressed she uttered the now immortal words "Maita'i roa ae!" which as you all know, means something like "The best!" or "Out of this world!" in Polynesian. The restaurant was called Trader Vic's, and the newly named Mai Tai became the best known of all Tiki cocktails.

However, Ernest Raymond Beaumont-Gantt, the owner of a new bar called Don the Beachcomber's, claimed that he invented the Mai Tai sometime in 1933 — albeit with a rather different recipe. Even if Trader Vic did "adapt" the Don the Beachcomber's recipe, the Mai Tai as we know it today is that of Trader Vic's.

As always, there is confusion with the recipe. Even Trader Vic had to change his own recipe, as the rum he originally used, 17 year old J. Wray and Nephew, all but ran out, mainly thanks to the popularity of the cocktail. There are apparently six bottles left of the 17 year old rum required, and the bar at the Merchant Hotel in Belfast, Northern Ireland, will use one to make you a Mai Tai for around $1,500. Below are listed Trader Vic's 1972 version, a.k.a. "Old Way", and the more modern formula.

"Old Way" Recipe

Ingredients

1 oz / 3 cl fine Jamaican rum (8 or 15 years old)
1 oz / 3 cl Martinique rum (preferably St James)
½ oz / 1½ cl Cointreau
¾ oz / 2¼ cl freshly squeezed lime juice (basically the juice of 1 lime)
½ oz / 1½ cl orgeat syrup (almond)

Preparation

• Shake all the ingredients with ice.
• Strain into a glass with crushed ice.
• Garnish with a sprig of mint.

Contemporary Recipe

Ingredients

Either
2 oz / 6 cl good aged rum
Or
1 oz / 3 cl gold rum
1 oz / 3 cl dark rum
And
½ oz / 1½ cl Cointreau
¾ oz / 2¼ cl freshly squeezed lime juice (basically the juice of 1 lime)
½ oz / 1½ cl orgeat syrup (almond)

Preparation

• Shake all the ingredients with ice.
• Strain into a glass with crushed ice.
• Garnish with a sprig of mint, pineapple wedge, cocktail cherry, and half the squeezed lime shell.

Mary Pickford

Glass
Cocktail

This cocktail is named after the Canadian silent film actress (ironically, known as America's Sweetheart) who, from around 1916 to the mid 1920's was just about the most famous celebrity in the world, with the exception of her good friend Charlie Chaplin. The Mary Pickford was (so the story goes...) invented especially for her, on a trip to Cuba with Fairbanks and Chaplin in the 1920's, by bartender Fred Kaufmann. As long as you don't overdo it with the sweeter ingredients, you'll have a surprisingly excellent cocktail.

Ingredients

2 oz / 6 cl white rum

1½ oz / 4½ cl freshly pressed
    pineapple juice

1 teaspoon grenadine syrup

1 teaspoon Maraschino liqueur

Preparation

• Shake all the ingredients
with ice.

• Double strain into a chilled glass.

• Garnish with a cocktail cherry.

Painkiller

Glass
Collins

A slightly weird, medicinal name, but this was a sailor's drink, and I suppose that after a long sea voyage, a few of these would ease both mind and body. It is believed that the Painkiller was invented at the fantastically named "Soggy Dollar Bar", on the island of Jost Van Dyke, in the British Virgin Islands. The bar is on a beach with a fiercely tricky to navigate coral reef; so, to this day, sailors anchor their boats on the reef and swim to the bar, and consequently the cash register is full of soggy dollars.

Ingredients

2 oz / 6 cl dark or Navy rum

2 oz / 6 cl freshly pressed
    pineapple juice

1 oz / 3 cl freshly squeezed
    orange juice

1 oz / 3 cl coconut cream

Preparation

• Shake all the ingredients
with ice.

• Strain into a glass filled with
crushed ice.

• Garnish with a pineapple wedge,
a pineapple leaf and a cocktail
cherry.

• Some sprinkle grated nutmeg on
the top.

Tom and Jerry

Glass
Toddy or Mug

This is one of the best cold weather drinks there is. While it was Professor Jerry Thomas who popularized the drink, it was, in fact, created by the sports writer Pierce Egan, who adapted an Eggnog recipe to publicize the 1821 launch of his book, entitled 'Life in London, or Days and Nights of Jerry Hawthorne and his Elegant Friend Corinthian Tom'. The Professor's recipe is well worth reading, although it's for making a large batch, and the first instruction is "Take 12 fresh eggs," which is enough to put anyone off!

Ingredients
1 egg
1½ oz / 4½ cl rum *
Pinch of ground cinnamon
Pinch of ground allspice
A few cloves
1 teaspoon of sugar
1 oz / 3 cl cognac
Hot water

Tip
* Today's recipes call for white or gold rum, but Thomas used Jamaica rum – such as Myers's, which I think adds a real depth of flavor.

Preparation
• Separate the egg and beat the white until stiff, and the yolk until thin.
• Transfer to the glass.
• Add the next five ingredients and stir – the texture should be like a light batter.
• Add the cognac, top with hot water, and stir.
• Grate nutmeg on top of the drink.

Zombie

Glass
Hurricane or Collins

You guessed it – drink too many of this cocktail and you will feel like a zombie. It is powerful stuff indeed! As with the Mai Tai, there was a bitter feud over the creation of this drink, involving our impressively named friend, Ernest Raymond Beaumont-Gantt (who eventually changed his name to Donn Beach), and another great American bartender, Patrick Gavin Duffy. Both claim to have invented a cocktail called a Zombie in the same year, 1934, although they are different drinks.

Ingredients
1½ oz / 4½ cl Barbados rum
  (such as Mountgay)
1½ oz / 4½ cl Jamaican rum
  (such as Myers's)
½ oz / 1½ cl Demerara 151
  Proof rum
1 oz / 3 cl freshly squeezed
  pressed pineapple juice
1 oz / 3 cl freshly squeezed
  lime juice
1 oz / 3 cl freshly squeezed
  lemon juice
1 bar spoon of brown sugar
½ oz / 1½ cl passion fruit syrup
Dash of Angostura Bitters

Preparation
• Stir sugar with lemon and lime juices in a shaker until dissolved.
• Add the rest of the ingredients except the Demerara rum, and shake with ice.
• Strain into a glass with crushed ice.
• Float the Demerara rum over the top.
• Garnish with a pineapple wedge and a sprig of mint.

Mojito

Perhaps the most refreshing cocktail of them all, the popularity of the Mojito outside of its natural Cuban home has grown dramatically over the last ten years. The ingredients are simple – rum, lime, sugar, mint and soda, although the techniques vary greatly. The history of the Mojito is unknown, but there are infinite theories. One such theory is that during Prohibition, visiting Americans brought the Mint Julep to the attention of the Cuban bartenders, or Cantineros, who in turn domesticated it with local products. Another theory is that Sir Francis Drake, the British Vice Admiral and favorite of Queen Elizabeth I, was partly responsible for bringing the the Mojito to Cuba! Drake attempted to plunder Cuba in the late 1570's and again in 1586, and while his attempts largely failed, a drink called "El Draque" appeared in 16th Century Cuba, being a medicinal combination of aguardiente (sugar cane liqueur), lime, mint and sugar (the last three ingredients were there to hide the taste of the liqueur, as much as for their medicinal value!). At some point, proper rum replaced the rough aguardiente and the name was changed to Mojito.

(continued on page 86)

Mojito

(continued from page 84)

Glass

Collins

Recipe 1
(Bodeguita del Medio)

Ingredients

1½ oz / 4½ cl white rum
   (Havana Club 3 Year Old)
Freshly squeezed lime juice
   (equivalent to half a lime)
2 teaspoons fine white sugar
2 sprigs of mint
3 oz / 9 cl soda water

Preparation

• Spoon the sugar into the glass.
• Add enough freshly squeezed
lime juice to cover the sugar.
• Add two sprigs of mint,
including stalks.*

• Add soda water.
• Lightly muddle the mint.
• Add the rum and four ice
cubes.**
• Stir and serve.

Tips

• This is such a simple, quick
drink that gives you a great result.
* At the legendary Havana bar,
La Bodeguita, they consider the
stalks essential to the flavor – see
what you think.
** No more, no less than four ice
cubes, and never crushed ice.

Recipe 2
(Contemporary)

Ingredients

2 oz / 6 cl rum
1 oz / 3 cl freshly squeezed
   lime juice
½ oz / 1½ cl sugar syrup
10–15 mint leaves
Soda water

Preparation

• Muddle the mint leaves gently in
the base of the glass.
• Add the rum, lime and sugar and
some crushed ice.
• Stir the drink well, churning all
the ingredients together.

• Fill the rest of the glass with
crushed ice and top off with soda
water.
• Garnish with a sprig of mint.

Tips

There is some debate as to
whether a couple of dashes of
Angostura Bitters should be
added. Personally, I don't – I like
the purity of the ingredients.
But try it for yourself and decide.

Above are three Mojito recipes, or styles. The first is from the Bodeguita del Medio, the second is the modern bartender's method, and the third is how I like to make them, plus some variations... When making a Mojito be careful with the mint. If you crush it too hard, the mint will turn bitter and discolor quickly, so be gentle.

The name Mojito could be derived from the African Voodoo term Mojo (a type of magic charm), which was also the name for a lime-based sauce, or from the Spanish 'mojadito,' meaning a little wet.

Recipe 3
(How I like it)

This is purely the way I like it, even though it's more work.
It's more in the style of a Caipirinha. For some, a clear drink is
more aesthetically pleasing, but in the case of the Mojito,
I love to see my glass packed full of green.

Ingredients

1 lime
2 bar spoons white sugar
Approximately 15 mint leaves
2 oz / 6 cl white rum
   (for me, Havana Club 3 Year Old)
Soda water

Preparation

• Cut the lime into 8 cubes.
• Muddle the lime with the sugar
in the metal part of a shaker.
• Hold the mint in one hand and
clap your hands together a few
times to release all the aromas,
add to the shaker and churn
a few times.
• Transfer the contents to a glass.
• Add the rum and some crushed
ice, stir and churn.
• Top off with crushed ice and
soda water and stir again.
• Garnish with a sprig of mint.

=== **Variations** ===

**Deluxe Mojito (a.k.a. Mojito
Royale) – use a fine, aged rum,
such as Havana Club 7 Year
Old or better, and substitute
champagne for the soda water.
Expensive, but oh so good!**

Variations

There are many different versions of Mojitos, especially
Fruit Mojitos. You can muddle some fruits into your drink,
for example strawberries work wonderfully, or add liqueurs
and fruit. One version I like is apple and hazelnut, but
experiment for yourself. Just decide how much fruit you
want in your drink.

Ingredients

½ cored green apple
10–15 mint leaves
1½ oz / 4½ cl white rum
½ oz / 1½ cl Frangelico
   (hazelnut liqueur)
1 oz / 3 cl freshly squeezed
   lime juice
1 oz / 3 cl freshly pressed
   apple juice
2 teaspoons white sugar
Soda water

Preparation

• Crush and muddle the apple in
the base of a shaker with
the sugar.
• Clap the mint between your
hands and stir in.
• Transfer the contents to
your glass.
• Add the rest of the ingredients
except the soda water.
• Add crushed ice, stir and
churn well.
• Top with crushed ice and
soda water.
• Garnish with a sprig of mint and
an apple slice.

Piña Colada

Piña Colada

Glass
Hurricane (if not, then a large Collins),
or of course, a frozen pineapple shell.

Ah the poor, maligned Piña Colada – the cocktail that serious bartenders sneer at or even refuse to make, and customers barely dare to order for fear of being ridiculed. When made very simply, it is a true Caribbean classic (and indeed a close relative of the Batidas of Brazil).

The expression Piña Colada has been around for a long time. It simply means 'pineapple strained,' and various drinks bearing the name can be found all over the Caribbean, and especially in Cuba, both with and without coconut, and with and without rum. But it is Puerto Rico that has claimed ownership of the drink, and since 1978, it has, in fact, been their national drink.

The most commonly accepted version of events is that Ramon "Monchito" Marrero created it at the Beachcomber Bar of the Caribe Hilton in San Jose, in 1954. Whatever you do, just don't start singing the Rupert Holmes 1979 hit, "Escape," which became known as the Piña Colada Song.

Ingredients
2 oz / 6 cl white rum
1½ oz / 4½ cl cream of coconut
4 oz / 12 cl freshly pressed
pineapple juice

Preparation
• Blend ingredients with crushed ice until smooth.
• Pour into glass and garnish with a pineapple wedge and a cocktail cherry.

─── Variations ───
If you prefer some texture to your drink, you can try blending the flesh of a pineapple and / or coconut – this will actually give you a Piña Sin Colar.

Planter's Punch

Glass

Collins

To many, punch is something served in a large bowl at a wedding or on prom night, that someone may or may not have spiked with cheap booze. To those who take their cocktails a little more seriously, there are strict rules and ratios to making a punch. The drink was invented by the founder of Myers's Rum, Fred L. Myers, at the end of the 19th Century, and for many years Myers's Rum bore the inscription "Planter's Punch Brand."

The classic Rum Punch formula is: 1 sour, 2 sweet, 3 strong, 4 weak – in this case: 1 lime juice, 2 sugar, 3 rum, 4 water. Myers called this the "Old Plantation" formula.

There is also an American Rum Punch formula: 1 sour, 2 sweet, 3 weak, 4 strong. Again, if you stick with the ratios of the formula, you can use any measurements (and ingredients for that matter).

Ingredients

½ oz / 1½ cl freshly squeezed lime juice

1 oz / 3 cl sugar syrup

1½ oz / 4½ cl Myers's rum

2 dashes of Angostura Bitters

2 oz / 6 cl mineral water

Preparation

• Shake the first four ingredients together with ice.

• Strain into a glass with ice and add mineral water.

• Garnish with an orange slice and a sprig of mint.

Variations

David Embury offers a different formula: 1 sweet, 2 sour, 3 strong, 4 weak.

You may see all manner of recipes using ingredients such as orange or pineapple juice, grenadine syrup, Triple Sec, white rum, lemon juice, pineapple garnish, cocktail cherry et cetera. All I will say is, it's your drink...

If you are going to experiment, try to stick to one of the formulas as a base – it will help you a lot.

Planter's Punch

Chimayó

Glass

Collins

The Chimayó was created in 1965, by Arturo Jaramillo, at the Rancho de Chimayó, in Chimayó, New Mexico. This is a curiously popular cocktail, and it even has its own Facebook page. It is, indeed, a very pleasant cocktail, a simple example of how tequila is rather more versatile than just mixing it with something sour...

Ingredients

1½ oz / 4½ cl gold tequila

1 oz / 3 cl freshly pressed
apple juice

¼ oz / ¾ cl freshly squeezed
lemon juice

¼ oz / ¾ cl Crème de Cassis

Preparation

• Shake all the ingredients with ice.

• Strain into a glass filled with ice.

• Garnish with a slice of apple.

El Diablo

Glass

Collins

Ah yes, the Devil. While its origins are not definite, it's probably a Trader Vic's creation. It first appeared in the 1946 Trader Vic's Book of Food and Drink under the name Mexican El Diablo. The Mexican seems to have been phased out over the years. A nice long drink to which you can add extra Tequila, if you're feeling frisky.

Ingredients

1½ oz / 4½ cl silver tequila

1 oz / 3 cl freshly squeezed
lime juice

½ oz / 1½ cl Crème de Cassis

Top with ginger ale

Tips

• I upped the lime juice to give it more bite – feel free to use less.

• I prefer ginger beer to ale, to add a bit of spice.

Preparation

• Shake the first three ingredients with ice.

• Strain into a glass filled with ice.

• Top with ginger ale.

• Drop in half a spent lime shell.

Rude Cosmopolitan

Glass
Cocktail

Silk Stockings

Glass
Champagne Flute or Martini

I could have stuck this in the Vodka and Gin Chapter as a variation to a Cosmopolitan – which it is, pure and simple. But I wanted you to see something... Look at the ingredients... Does that look like a Cosmo to you? Hmmm, well, kind of yes. Now take another look. Does that not look like a Margarita shaded with cranberry juice? What is this drink? A Cosmo or a Margarita? Or both? A Cosmarita?

This is a curiously delightful after-dinner cocktail. It tastes great, but you just don't expect your tequila to taste of creamy chocolate and berries.

Ingredients
1½ oz / 4½ cl tequila
1 oz / 3 cl Cointreau
1 oz / 3 cl freshly squeezed
  lime juice
1½ oz / 4½ cl cranberry juice

Preparation
• Shake all the ingredients
with ice.
• Double strain into a chilled glass.
• Flame an orange twist over the
drink, wipe around the rim of the
glass, and drop inside.

Tips
• Make sure you use good quality
cranberry juice.
• It's hard to find, but a few drops
of orange bitters really gives it
a lift.
• If you find the drink a bit harsh,
change the recipe to 2 oz / 6 cl of
cranberry juice.

Recommendations
• As with the original
Cosmopolitan, what could be
ruder than adding a nice piece of
muddled ginger?
• You can, of course, serve this
drink with a salt rim if you so
desire.

Ingredients
1½ oz / 4½ cl tequila
¾ oz / 2¼ cl white Crème de Cacao
½ oz / 1½ cl Chambord liqueur
1 oz / 3 cl heavy cream

Preparation
• Shake all the ingredients
with ice.
• Strain into a chilled glass.
• Sprinkle ground cinnamon
on top.

Margarita

Even though a relative youngster in the world of cocktails, this lip-smacking, sour concoction is already shrouded in myth; no one really knows when, where, or who invented it, or even what the exact, original recipe is... Here are some of the most popular stories, and believe me, these are just two:

• Probably the most famous story involves the socialite Margaret Sames, who used to host fabulous parties for "The Team" at her house in Acapulco. When you consider that "The Team" included John Wayne, Lana Turner and Nicky Hilton, you can understand why this is the most well known version. Margaret came up with the drink at her 1948 Christmas party.

• Rita Hayworth is also associated with the invention of the Margarita. She is supposed to have inspired more than one bartender to make a drink and call it after her. And her name before she became Rita Hayworth? Margarita Cansino.

You need to decide how you like your Margarita —how sour? What ratio? Straight up, on the rocks, crushed ice, or frozen? Table salt, rock salt, no salt? Here are some options.

(continued on page 96)

Margarita

(continued from page 94)

Glass
Margarita* (straight up) or Old-Fashioned (with ice)

Ingredients
2 oz / 6 cl tequila (your choice)
¾ oz / 2¼ cl Cointreau
1 oz / 3 cl freshly squeezed
    lime juice

Preparation
• Prepare your glass with a rim of salt (optional), being careful not to get any on the inside of the glass.
• Shake the ingredients with ice.
• Double strain into a Margarita glass or strain into a glass with ice.
• Garnish with a wedge of lime (optional).

Tips
* If you don't have a Margarita glass, just use a cocktail glass and some attitude.
• As I said – feel free to change the measurements as you wish. There's something quite harsh about a Margarita that I like – the shock of the sourness, and the faint burn of the tequila.
• Rock or sea salt can look messy, but I rather like it in a rustic sort of way. The bigger crystals dissolve more slowly and thus have less impact than table salt. If you prefer, grind it down with a mortar and pestle to make it finer.
• I usually rim just half of the glass with salt, meaning you can take or leave the salt as you wish.
• I normally drink a Margarita straight up, so I don't really have an opinion on crushed or cubed ice.

Options
• A 3 tequila: 2 Cointreau: 1 lime ratio is a very popular, and more common recipe:
1½ oz / 4½ cl tequila
1 oz / 3 cl Cointreau
½ oz / 1½ cl freshly squeezed
    lime juice

• **Sweeter** – You can lessen the lime and increase the Cointreau, or add a dash of sugar syrup of you prefer a less sour drink. Alternatively, you can find Agave Nectar in many shops these days, and it will enhance the flavor of a Margarita much more than plain old sugar.

• **Smoother** – Some like to add a dash of egg white to the shaker to make the cocktail smoother, and I fully recommend it; it gives a straight up Margarita extra body.

• **Frozen** – You can, of course, blend it with crushed ice, to get a Frozen Margarita – personally I'm not a big fan, as the chill detracts from the taste. You may want to add sugar in this case, and be careful not to add too much ice, or you'll just lose the taste altogether.

1942 - Fransisco "Pancho" Morales, a bartender in Ciudad Juarez, Mexico, was asked by a lady for a Magnolia. As he couldn't quite remember the recipe (brandy, egg yolk and Curaçao) he made up something on the spot, and named it Margarita. Some say Pancho named it Margarita after the lady who loved her new drink, others that the name is that of another flower, a daisy.

Glass

Margarita

Melon Margarita

Here's a recipe for a Melon Margarita. The basic premise is to substitute a fresh muddled fruit and its liqueur or syrup, or just sugar, for the Cointreau, which is the sweetening agent in this cocktail. You'll have to decide if you want a salt rim or not...

Variations

Like the Caiprinha, and the Daiquiri, the Margarita has spawned endless variations. You may have noticed that these simple drinks, consisting of liqueur, lime, and a touch of sweetness, lend themselves to be built on. There are some great simple Fruit Margaritas, and in the last few years especially, bartenders have really begun pushing the boundaries with ingredients (for better and for worse). Fresh herbs and spices, such as sage and lavender, cardamom and obviously ginger, are just a few examples. I am a fan of making Margaritas with infused tequila, some of my favorite flavors being cinnamon, vanilla, ginger, chili, grapefruit (made with the peel) and coffee.

Ingredients

A good sized chunk of ripe, seasonal melon

2 oz / 6 cl tequila

1 oz / 3 cl melon liqueur / schnapps or Midori

1 oz / 3 cl freshly squeezed lime juice

Preparation

• If you're going to use salt, prepare your glass.

• Muddle the melon in the base of the shaker.

• Add the rest of the ingredients and shake with ice.

• Double strain into a chilled glass.

• Garnish with a slice of melon.

Options

• I have a confession... I've always known a drink by the name of a Japanese Slipper to be a Melon Margarita without fresh melon. While doing my research, I discovered that I'm quite wrong. Let's just say that a Japanese Slipper is as above, but without the fresh melon, and with a salt rim.

• Oh, the "real" Japanese Slipper is equal measures of Midori, Cointreau and lime juice.

Whisky & Brandy

Cocktails

Whisky has been distilled in some form for a thousand years. There were definitely distilleries in Ireland in the 12th Century, if not before. The word itself comes from Gaelic, and is derived from the Latin term Aqua Vitae; in Irish Gaelic 'uisce beatha' and in the Scottish 'uisge beatha' – uisce / ge' translating as water (just as vodka takes its name from the Russian and Polish for water). There are so many different types of whisky in production today, and the production of most falls under strict governmental legislation. You need to choose your whiskies carefully for cocktails.

Brandy, as we know it today, was actually discovered quite by accident. Since transporting wine was a costly business, and was taxed by volume, merchants began to distil their wines for travel, storing them in oak barrels, thus greatly reducing their bulk and costs. The idea was to add water back to the distilled wine, once it arrived at its destination. However, it was discovered that the product in those barrels was rather good, better in fact than the product from which it had been distilled. There are a lot of great Brandy cocktails out there, and particularly in the U.S.A., Applejack is a great alternative to cognac, and indeed, for some, to whisky, and much less expensive. When I use the general term brandy, unless I specify otherwise, I'm referring to brandy distilled from wine.

Algonquin

Glass
Cocktail

The Algonquin Hotel was the venue for the daily meeting in the Oak Room of the legendary Algonquin Round Table. In 1987 it was granted status as a New York City historic landmark, largely owing to its long association with notable figures of literature and the theater. This is a fairly easy way to ease us into whisky drinks. The recipe is quite specific about certain ingredients, but be grateful, as the Algonquin has another well known house cocktail, the Martini on the Rock, which will cost you $10,000; the rock in question is a 1.52 carat diamond.

Ingredients
2 oz / 6 cl rye whisky
1 oz / 3 cl Noilly Prat dry
   vermouth *
1 oz / 3 cl freshly pressed
   pineapple juice
1 dash Angostura Bitters

Preparation
• Shake all the ingredients
with ice.
• Double strain into a chilled glass.
• Garnish with a cocktail cherry.

Tips
* The recipe specifies Noilly Prat. It is a fine vermouth, and I strongly recommend it as your default dry vermouth.
• Some recipes serve this drink in an Old Fashioned, on the rocks.

Blood and Sand

Glass
Cocktail

Despite all my talk about retaining the flavor and integrity of the liqueur I love this drink. It's an absolutely perfect example of how a story can sell a drink. In 1922 one of the greatest silent movies of the era was released, the critically acclaimed Blood and Sand, starring Rudolph Valentino, the original heart throb. The cocktail was made for the release of the film, its color reminiscent of the bloodied surface of the bullfighting arena. This is a great drink. It's rich, complex, fruity and smoky and has a delightful froth.

Ingredients
¾ oz / 2¼ cl blended Scotch
   whisky
¾ oz / 2¼ cl red vermouth
   (preferably Punt e Mes)
¾ oz / 2¼ cl Cherry Heering
   (or cherry brandy)
¾ oz / 2¼ cl freshly squeezed
   orange juice

Preparation
• Shake all the ingredients
with ice.
• Double strain into a chilled glass.
• Garnish with a twist of orange.

Tip
If by chance you find this recipe too sweet, increase the amount of Scotch and decrease the rest.

Bobby Burns

Glass
Cocktail

It is commonly believed that this fine drink is named in honor of the Scottish bard, 18th Century poet Robert Burns, who in 2009 was officially voted the Greatest Scot of all time by the Scottish public. The cocktail appeared in three cocktail books, Harry Craddock's 'The Savoy Cocktail Book' of 1930, Albert Steven's Crockett's 'The Old Waldorf-Astoria Bar Book' of 1931, and David Embury's 'The Fine Art of Mixing Drinks' of 1948, and is, of course, different in each one. Below is Craddock's recipe for this deeply herbal, luscious cocktail.

Ingredients
2 oz / 6 cl Scotch whisky
1 oz / 3 cl sweet vermouth
¼ oz / ¾ cl Benedictine DOM

Preparation
• Stir all the ingredients with ice 52 times.
• Double strain into a chilled glass.
• Spray the oil from a lemon twist over the drink, wipe around the rim of the glass, and drop in as a garnish.

Tips
• The original recipe called for equal parts of Scotch and sweet vermouth, but this is rather on the sweet side. If you do prefer a sweeter drink, adjust accordingly.
• Note that this is almost like a Rob Roy with herbal flavors.

═══ **Variations** ═══
**David Embury replaced the Benedictine with Drambuie liqueur, and added a few dashes of Peychaud bitters.
Also very nice.**

Lynchburg Lemonade

Glass
Collins

Lynchburg is the home of one of the biggest brand names in the world, Jack Daniel's. The Lynchburg Lemonade was created by Tony Mason, a restaurant-bar owner from Alabama. Mason claimed that a Jack Daniel's sales representative, Winston Randle, took the recipe back with him to the distillery, whereupon Jack Daniel's began using it for their own campaign without acknowledging Mason in any way. In 1987 Mason sued the Distillery for misappropriation of his trade secret, and actually won! Mason was after $13 million in damages, but the judge awarded him the princely sum of $1.

Ingredients
1½ oz / 4½ cl Jack Daniel's
1 oz / 3 cl Triple Sec or Cointreau
1 oz / 3 cl freshly squeezed lemon juice
Top with lemon-lime soda (such as 7-Up or Sprite)

Preparation
• Shake the first three ingredients with ice.
• Strain into a glass with ice.
• Top with lemon-lime soda.
• Garnish with a wedge of lemon.

Hot Toddy

Glass

Toddy or Mug

Every bartender knows that there's no such thing as a cure for the common cold, but this drink has to be pretty close – or at least it will give you a good night's sleep and some respite. It is usually made with Scottish whisky (single malt for purists, blended Scotch for those of us who can't afford to be so pure).

No one really knows where the drink or the name came from. All you need to know is that as soon as you feel a cold coming on you should drink one of these and go straight to bed.

Ingredients

2 oz / 6 cl Scotch whisky

1 bar spoon of sugar or honey

A wedge of lemon

A few cloves

A cinnamon stick

Hot water

Preparation

• Rinse out the glass with hot water.

• Mix all the ingredients in the glass, adding the hot water last, and stir.

• Sprinkle grated nutmeg on top.

Tips

• While this drink is "medicinal" in nature, don't mix it with any medicine you are taking.

• Although I think the drink works perfectly as it is, you could also add other spices should you feel so inclined. Ginger helps if you are feeling nauseous.

Alternatives

Hot Toddy is usually made with Scotch whisky, but obviously, you could substitute it for other liqueurs, such as:

Other types of whisky

Rum

Brandy

Applejack

Gin

Hot Toddy

Irish Coffee

Irish Coffee

Glass
Toddy or Mug

This classic after-dinner drink was invented in 1943 at Foynes Airport in County Limerick, Ireland. Foynes was a small refueling stop-off on the early commercial New York to Southampton flights. Back then, the Boeing 314 "Clipper" flying boats flew at around 160 mph, and a flight from Botwood, Newfoundland, could take anything from 12 to 17 hours, depending on the winds. A return ticket cost $675, which back then was something only the very rich could afford. The restaurant that catered to these customers at Foynes was, therefore, considered one of the best in Ireland. The story goes that one winter night the captain of the flight from Foynes to Botwood decided to turn back due to severe weather. The restaurant staff was asked to prepare food and drink for the tired and freezing passengers, and the chef, Joe Sheridan, decided to slip a little extra something into their coffees. When one of the delighted passengers asked Sheridan if the coffee was Brazilian, he replied "no, that's Irish Coffee..." The drink traveled to America courtesy of Pulitzer Prize winning travel writer Stanton Delaplane, who fell in love with the drink from Foynes. He and the owners of the Buena Vista Cafe in San Francisco spent months perfecting their recipe. Thanks to Delaplane's newspaper column the drink became a huge hit, and the Buena Vista alone made over 30 million Irish Coffees (by their count) until they got sick of them.

Ingredients

2 oz / 6 cl Irish whisky
Hot black coffee (good percolated – not instant!)
Heavy cream
1 bar spoon white or brown sugar (minimum)

Preparation

• Shake the cream in a container or shaker, or whisk until lightly whipped but still runny.
• Rinse the glass with hot water, and place the bar spoon inside.
• Add the whisky, sugar and coffee and stir.
• Carefully float the cream over the back of the bar spoon onto the top of the coffee, to a thickness of about ½ inch.

Tips

• It will help if the cream is not cold from the refrigerator but closer to room temperature.
• The cream should not be whipped too much, but the thicker it is the easier it is to float.
• The sugar gives the coffee viscosity, which helps the cream to float. You need a minimum of one spoonful of sugar.
• When pouring the cream, the spoon should be virtually touching the surface of the coffee so that it slides on, rather than drops in.

Variations
You can make endless versions of Irish Coffee, by replacing the whisky with a different liqueur, for example, rum, cognac, Galliano, Crème de Cacao, coffee liqueur, Irish Cream, ad infinitum.

Manhattan

For many, this is The Cocktail – and for those who disagree it is often the benchmark by which they judge what is their favorite. Complete complex sophistication in a glass. Along with the Mint Julep and the Old Fashioned, the Manhattan is one of the best expressions of American bar culture.

The most popular myth was, until recently, that the Manhattan was created at the Manhattan Club in November 1874, at a banquet hosted by Lady Randolph Churchill for Samuel Tilden, the newly elected Governor of New York. However, David Wondrich, the excellent cocktail historian, has pointed out that Lady Randolph was not in New York at that time, but rather at home, giving birth to her son, Winston Churchill. So, no cocktail for the Governor then. Wondrich believes that the cocktail was probably invented at the Manhattan Club in the 1870's.

The Manhattan comes in three versions, Sweet, Perfect and Dry – for me personally a Manhattan is Sweet, and the other two are variations. And get out the good stuff for this one. This needs good whisky, and while you'll read that this whisky is better for a Manhattan, or that vermouth is worse, it is up to you and your taste, and no one else.

Glass
Cocktail

Sweet

Ingredients
2 oz / 6 cl rye whisky or bourbon*
1 oz / 3 cl sweet vermouth**
1 or 2 dashes of Angostura Bitters
A few drops of Maraschino
    liqueur (optional)***

Preparation
• Stir the ingredients 52 times in
a mixing glass with ice.
• Double strain into a chilled glass.
• Spray the oil from an orange
twist over the drink, wipe around
the rim of the glass, and discard.
• Garnish with a cocktail cherry.

Tips
* Manhattans were originally
made with rye, but bourbon,
which is a bit sweeter, seems
more popular today. I personally
make mine with Woodford
Reserve Bourbon. Having
said that, rye is making a big
comeback, in popularity and
quality.
** I recommend Punt e Mes.
*** Some use a few drops of the
liqueur from a jar of cocktail
cherries. We've all done it, but
it's kind of cheap. If you've got
Maraschino liqueur in the house,
use that.
• It became the fashion recently
to garnish with two cocktail
cherries, in honor of 9/11.

Perfect

Ingredients
2 oz / 6 cl rye whisky or bourbon
½ oz / 1½ cl sweet vermouth
½ oz / 1½ cl dry vermouth
1 or 2 dashes of Angostura Bitters

Preparation
• Stir the ingredients 52 times in
a mixing glass with ice.
• Double strain into a chilled glass.
• Spray the oil from a lemon twist
over the drink, wipe around the
rim of the glass, and discard.
• Garnish with a cocktail cherry.

Dry

Ingredients
2 oz / 6 cl rye whisky or bourbon
1 oz / 3 cl dry vermouth
1 or 2 dashes of Angostura Bitters

Preparation
• Stir the ingredients 52 times in
a mixing glass with ice.
• Double strain into a chilled glass.
• Spray the oil from an lemon
twist over the drink, wipe around
the rim of the glass, and drop into
the glass.

=== **Variations** ===
Champagne Manhattan
**a Sweet Manhattan topped
with champagne**
Rob Roy – **a Sweet Manhattan
made with Scotch whisky**
Brandy Manhattan – **a Sweet
Manhattan made with cognac
instead of whisky.**

Mint Julep

Glass
Julep Cup or Old Fashioned

This is an exceptionally fine drink when made well, and dull, bordering on the unpleasant (somewhat like stewed tea) when made badly – and it's a fine line, so be careful. As is so often the case, its simplicity is the downfall of many a bartender. No one knows where the Julep originates from exactly, but it's definitely more than 200 years old, first appearing in print in 1803 (although it was mentioned by the likes of John Milton and Dr Samuel Johnson as a cordial).The word Julep is derived from the Persian 'gulab' meaning 'rose water,' an ancient Persian drink of water, sugar and rose petals.

Personally, I think the cocktail version goes back to Colonial days, as historically Juleps were made with either brandy or rum, as well as bourbon. For this reason also, a Bourbon Mint Julep is often referred to as either a Kentucky or Southern Mint Julep, to distinguish it from other recipes. Since 1938 the Mint Julep has been the official drink of the Kentucky Derby. As always, for such a simple drink, there are a hundred ways to make it.

Then comes the zenith of man's pleasure. Then comes the julep – the mint julep. Who has not tasted one has lived in vain. The honey of Hymettus brought no such solace to the soul; the nectar of the Gods is tame beside it. It is the very dream of drinks, the vision of sweet quaffings.

Joshua Soule Smith, Kentucky Colonel, from The Lexington Herald, 1880's

Ingredients

2 oz / 6 cl bourbon*
½ oz – ¾ oz / 1½ cl – 2¼ cl sugar
   syrup
4 sprigs of mint

Preparation

• Chill your cup.
• Gently muddle the mint with the sugar syrup in the cup.**
• Almost fill the cup with finely crushed ice, or even better, shaved ice.
• Add the bourbon, stir and churn.
• Pack the rest of the cup with ice.
• Garnish with a sprig of mint.***

Tips

* Obviously it's up to you, but use a good bourbon because the ice will dilute the drink and the bite of the bourbon as well. I personally like Woodford Reserve, but if you're looking for something a bit more powerful then try the Jim Beam Small Batch collection (Knob Creek, Booker's and Baker's).

** As with the Mojito, it is vital not to crush the mint, which will cause it to be bitter. I crush the mint between my hands instead of muddling, and then lightly press it into the sugar syrup (you're actually making mint syrup).

*** Other optional garnishes include a slice of orange and a pineapple spear (which you can use as a stirrer).

• Some people add Angostura Bitters to their Mint Juleps, but it upsets the harmony of the drink. Try with and without, and see what you think.

• A Mint Julep should really be made with spearmint (Mentha Spicata) – but don't worry too much about it.

• If you are drinking from a Julep cup hold it by the bottom or the rim. Holding it by the sides will ruin the frost.

• This is one drink where I prefer to use sugar syrup rather than granulated or powdered sugar.

Recommendations

You can also prepare your Mint Julep ahead of time, which some people swear is better (others will happily shoot you for it). Place the ingredients in the cup without ice, and refrigerate overnight, steeping the mint in the bourbon, and maximizing the flavors. All you have to do is add ice – but remember that it's already cold, and you won't get any dilution from the melting ice – so I recommend you add a splash of water.

Variations

Juleps can also be made by replacing the bourbon by rye whisky, rum, brandy or applejack.

A Georgia Mint Julep uses 1½ oz / 4½ cl brandy (or bourbon) and 1½ oz / 4½ cl apricot brandy.

Mint Julep

Old Fashioned

Glass
Old Fashioned

This is a tricky one to get right, but if you do, the result is sublime, and a triumph of simplicity. But make an Old Fashioned with a rye or bourbon you love, or not at all.

The myth goes that it was created at the Pendennis Club, Louisville, Kentucky, in the 1880's, for Colonel James E. Pepper, who then may have taken the recipe with him to the bar of the Waldorf-Astoria in New York, and brought it fame. However, David Wondrich pointed out that the Chicago Tribune actually mentions the Old Fashioned in 1880, and the Pendennis Club was founded in 1881...In the 1862 edition of Professor Jerry Thomas' guide, he lists a 'Whisky Cocktail,' which is just about the same as an Old Fashioned. The common belief nowadays is that the name is derived from the order of a "Whisky Cocktail, (the) old-fashioned (way)." Just as the glass became an Old Fashioned, so did the popular drink that went in it.

I'll give you a couple of ways to make it, basically the English way, and the American way. Take your time with it. The ice should melt into the drink to dilute it slightly. There is also a sugar debate. A sugar cube is the perfect amount of sugar, although you have to make certain it dissolves completely. Sugar syrup is also fine, although harder to measure.

Ingredients

Either

1 white sugar cube doused with 3 dashes of Angostura Bitters

A splash of water (same amount as sugar)

Or

½ oz / 1½ cl sugar syrup

And

3 dashes of Angostura Bitters

2 oz / 6 cl bourbon (even 3 oz / 9 cl if you like)

A twist of orange*

Preparation

This method is used by many bartenders in Britain, and is based on the Deluxe variation of David Embury. It takes a long time, but ensures perfect dilution.
Either

• Place the sugar cube in the base of the glass, douse with Angostura Bitters, add a splash of water, and muddle until the sugar is dissolved (use the muddler and glass as you would a mortar and pestle).

Or

• Add the sugar syrup and Angostura Bitters to the glass.

Then

• Add 2 ice cubes and stir for about a minute.

• Add another 2 ice cubes and stir for about a minute.

• Add 1 oz / 3 cl bourbon (or 1½ oz / 4½ cl).

• Squeeze the oil from an orange twist into the glass.

• Add 2 ice cubes and stir for about a minute.

• Add another 2 ice cubes and stir for about a minute.

• Add another 1 oz / 3 cl bourbon (or 1½ oz / 4½ cl) and 2 ice cubes, and stir for about a minute.

• Add ice to near the top of the glass, squeeze the twist again, wipe around the rim of the glass, drop inside, and stir.

Tips

• Yes, it does take about 7 minutes if you do it properly, but it's worth it!

• Some people muddle wedges of orange or lemon into the drink. Please, don't do that. This probably came from Prohibition when the fruit was used to hide the roughness of the liqueur.

• Some people top the drink with soda or even 7-Up. Uh uh. Seriously, we're not kids anymore.

• Some people muddle a cocktail cherry into the drink. What???

* While a twist of lemon is technically the more correct garnish, most bartenders use orange today, and it's so much better.

• Go easy with the sugar and bitters. You can always add more if you need.

The American method is simpler:

Either

• Place the sugar cube in the base of the glass, douse with Angostura Bitters, add a splash of water, and muddle until the sugar is dissolved (use the muddler and glass as you would a mortar and pestle).

Or

• Add the sugar syrup and Angostura Bitters to the glass.

Then

• Fill half the glass with ice, add 1 oz / 3 cl bourbon (or 1½ oz / 4½ cl) and stir well.

• Squeeze the oil from an orange twist into the glass.

• Add more ice and another 1 oz / 3 cl bourbon (or 1½ oz / 4½ cl) and stir well.

• Add ice to near the top of the glass, squeeze the twist again, wipe around the rim of the glass, drop inside, and stir.

Optional

You could try using other sweeteners such as maple syrup or honey, but be careful. I've never quite been satisfied with the results when trying this. With maple syrup, for example, if you add enough to get a real taste of maple, you've already added too much.

═══ Variations ═══

Treacle an outstanding take on the Old Fashioned, by the one and only Dick Bradsell. Using the English method above, substitute Dark Jamaican Rum, such as Myers's, for the whisky. Your last step, however, after you've finished stirring, should be to add just ½ oz / 1½ cl of freshly pressed apple juice. Simple and divine!

Old Fashioned

American Beauty

Glass

Cocktail

This is a rather odd cocktail, delicious, but odd. First of all, very little is known about it, other than it might have gotten its name from the American Beauty Rose, rather than the film or the Grateful Dead album of the same name. Secondly, it uses both Crème de Menthe and orange juice. There are several recipes – all use the same ingredients, but have different measurements. This is a very sophisticated drink, but I suggest you play around with the measurements to suit your taste.

Ingredients

½ oz / 1½ cl cognac

½ oz / 1½ cl dry vermouth

½ oz / 1½ cl freshly squeezed
    orange juice

1 teaspoon grenadine syrup

1 teaspoon Crème de Menthe
    (white)

Float of Port

Preparation

• Shake the first five ingredients with ice.

• Double strain into a chilled glass.

• Carefully float a small amount of port over the top of the drink (no more than ¼ oz / ¾ cl).

Tips

• I prefer to use more cognac, say 1 oz / 3cl, but that's me.

• Obviously, if you just happen to have an American Beauty sitting in a vase somewhere, one petal would make an amazing garnish (just don't let anyone eat it!).

• It might be interesting to experiment with a heavy red wine instead of the Port (which is a nice way of saying 'if you don't have any Port...').

Brandy

Brandy can also refer to liqueurs made from other kinds of fruit such as Applejack and Calvados, Schnapps, Slivowitz, and a whole range of Rakia; there is also Pomace Brandy, such as Grappa, or the Middle Eastern Arak, and the Raki of Turkey, and the Raki of the Balkans; and there is the mighty Pisco from either Chile or Peru (well, both, but it's a very sore point between the two countries). These are not to be confused with Liqueurs; Fruit Brandies tend to be clear, owing to the process of distillation, and are actually a form of Eau de Vie (water of life).

American Beauty

Brandy Alexander

Glass

Cocktail

The Brandy Alexander is a superb after dinner drink. Although it was actually created in 1922 for the wedding of Mary, Princess Royal and Viscount Lascelles, it was wildly popular in the 1970's, and now seems to be making a welcome comeback. The Brandy Alexander was adapted from the Alexander, a 1915 similar drink based on gin.

Cognac falls into various ascending categories, determined by age, which in turn, determines quality and price. A cognac product is normally a blend of different brandies from the region of Cognac and the age is determined by the youngest brandy within the blend. The following ages are the absolute minimum required by law, but they are normally much older, as cognac only improves with age.

VS Very Special – Aged at least two and a half years in cask
VSOP Very Superior (or Special) Old Pale – Aged at least four and a half years oak in cask
XO Extra Old – Aged at least 6 and a half years in cask (but normally much longer, say 20 years)
Napoleon* – Aged at least six and a half years in cask
Vieille Reserve and **Hors D'Âge** – A grade after XO, the latter meaning Beyond Age (and my wallet)

* Napoleon – be careful: you can find very cheap Napoleon brandies, but don't think you just got the bargain of a lifetime – it's cheap for a reason. Good for cooking... Just a few days ago I saw a bottle of "Napoleon XO Special Reserve Cognac" – for about $15. Hmmm.

If you're serious about your cognac cocktails, find a reasonably priced VSOP and use that. If you're not sure, then by all means use a VS to experiment, but bear in mind that your drinks will only improve the older you go.

Ingredients
1 oz / 3 cl cognac
1 oz / 3 cl brown / dark Crème
   de Cacao
1 oz / 3 cl heavy cream

Tip
For a bit of a kick, you can add more brandy – I do.

Preparation
• Shake the ingredients well
with ice.
• Double strain into a chilled glass.
• Sprinkle grated nutmeg over
the top.

Brandy Alexander

Champagne Cocktails

05

Champagne

Cocktails

Legend has it that a certain Dom Pierre Pérignon, a Benedictine monk and cellar master of the Hautvilliers Abbey, near Épernay, invented champagne quite by accident. The wines of Champagne had always been somewhat pale in comparison to other red wines, perhaps because the cool climate prevented proper fermentation while the juice was still in contact with the skins. Since the wine was bottled before the fermentation process had fully converted all the sugars to alcohol, there was residual sugar inside the bottle. Come spring, the natural yeasts that still remained in the bottle would wake up with the warmer weather, producing carbon dioxide as a by-product. The alarming result was exploding bottles, which prompted the monks to call it "devil's wine." Dom Pérignon tried to get rid of the bubbles by removing the skins from the grapes before fermentation hoping that this would alter the chemistry. Unfortunately the bubbles were still there, but when he tasted the resulting, sparkling, straw colored wine, he is said to have called out: "Brothers, come quickly! I'm tasting stars."

Bellini

Glass
Flute

This is a damn fine drink, simple, fresh, and utterly delightful, which is something that people tend to forget when they think of Bellinis. The key is the ingredients.

A true Bellini consists of only two ingredients, white peach purée and Prosecco, a dry, white, Italian sparkling wine. You can make white peach purée by peeling and squeezing fresh, ripe white peaches, and by gently pressing some of the flesh – don't use a blender, as it aerates the purée too much. Add a dash of sugar syrup if the peaches are a bit sour, but you shouldn't have to. If you have to use something other than Prosecco, make sure it's dry and light.

The Bellini was invented in 1945 by Giuseppe Cipriani, owner of Harry's Bar in Venice. It is named after the 15th Century Venetian painter Giovanni Bellini, apparently because the color of the drink was, to Cipriani, reminiscent of the particular shade of pink that the painter used for the toga of a saint in one of his works. Harry's Bar had many famous regular customers, including Charlie Chaplin, Orson Welles, and Truman Capote. The Bellini was a particular favorite of none other than Ernest Hemingway who was writing Over the River and Into the Trees in Venice in 1949–50, and mentioned Harry's Bar several times in the work.

Ingredients

⅓ white peach purée
⅔ oz / 2 cl Prosecco

Preparation

• Add the peach purée to the glass.
• Slowly and carefully add the Prosecco – it will foam up a lot! Stir gently.
• Garnish with a peach slice.

Tip

Many use peach schnapps / brandy / liqueur or Crème de Pêche. Try not to, although a good quality Crème de Pêche is preferable if you absolutely must.

=== Variations ===

These days there are all sorts of flavored "Bellinis." As always, I'll leave you to decide on that. Obviously, red berries such as strawberries and particularly raspberries would work well – but I beg you, hold off on the sugar! Or at least go easy. It doesn't have to be sickly sweet. For an extra kick, there is a drink sometimes known as a Metropolis (see under Russian Spring Punch, page 129):

1 oz / 3 cl vodka
1 oz / 3 cl strawberry purée
½ oz / 1½ cl Crème de Framboise (strawberry liqueur)
Top off with champagne.

Bellini

Black Velvet

Black Velvet

Glass
Flute

The Black Velvet was created in 1861 at the Brook's Club in London. On December 14th Queen Victoria's husband Prince Albert died, and to match the black armbands that the British public were wearing as a mark of condolence, the bar steward of the club turned the champagne black by adding stout beer. The grief-stricken Queen wore black for the rest of her life, so devastated was she by the death of her beloved Albert.

There is some confusion over what type of glass it should be served in, and many say a British pint glass, or a Collins. However, if it really was invented as a way to serve mourning champagne, then it should be served in a champagne glass. True, you'll have to refill it more often, but at least it won't go warm, as it would in a pint glass.

Ingredients
½ glass of good stout beer, preferably Guinness
Top off with champagne

Preparation
• Pour the stout in first and carefully add the champagne

Tip
There is some talk of floating one ingredient on top of the other, which I frankly find ridiculous.

=== **Variations** ===

There are several variations of the Black Velvet, such as Poor Man's Black Velvet, which mixes cider and stout, instead of champagne.
I sometimes add ½ oz / 1½ cl of Chambord Liqueur, to make what I call a Royal Velvet, and to add an interesting fruit twist.

"I drink it when I'm happy and when I'm sad
Sometimes, I drink it when I'm alone
When I have company I consider it obligatory.
I trifle with it if I'm not hungry and drink it if I am
Otherwise I never touch it - unless I'm thirsty."

Madame Lily Bollinger (1884 – 1977) – one of the 'Great Dames' of Champagne

Classic Champagne Cocktail

Glass
Flute

The true Champagne Cocktail is an old drink indeed, going back to the original recipe of a Cocktail, as first published in 1806 – liqueur, sugar, bitters and water. In this case, we simply have champagne, sugar and bitters, with a twist of lemon. This version appears in print as early as 1855. It is mentioned in Mark Twain's 'The Innocents Abroad' of 1869, and the recipe is given in the first edition, 1862, of Jerry Thomas' The Bartender's Guide, as a Champagne Cocktail, along with Brandy Cocktail, Whisky Cocktail and so on. The recipe is simple: douse a sugar cube in Angostura Bitters, place in the glass, and top off with chilled champagne. Add a lemon or orange twist (or both) and a lump of ice. Water is not required.

However, in 1899, a barman named John Dougherty won the New York Cocktail Competition with a cocktail he called the Business Brace. The drink has been popular ever since, although its name quickly changed, and it has often been confused with the original Champagne Cocktail.

Classic Champagne Cocktail

Ingredients
½ oz – 1oz / 1½ cl – 3cl cognac
1 lump of sugar soaked in
    Angostura Bitters
Top off with champagne

Preparation
• Douse the sugar cube with a few dashes of Angostura Bitters and drop in the glass.
• Add enough cognac to cover the sugar.
• Carefully top off with champagne.
• Garnish with a curled lemon twist.

Optional
• For an Old Champagne Cocktail, simply omit the cognac.
• Some bartenders also add a dash of Grand Marnier to the Classic Champagne Cocktail – no more than ½ oz / 1½ cl, if you want to try it.

There is no getting away from the prestige and allure of champagne, or the price for that matter. From personal experience, I advise you not to even taste something like a Krug Clos de Mesnil, and definitely not Clos D'Ambonnay Grand Cru, unless you have access to a regular supply; once you drink something of this quality, it's almost impossible to go back to 'everyday' champagne.

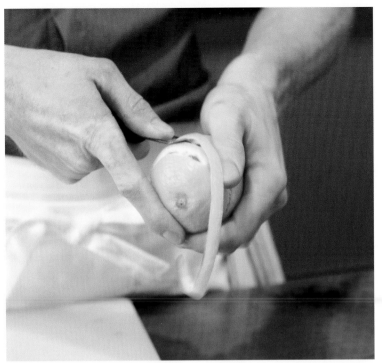

Classic Champagne Cocktail

French 75

Glass
Flute

Oh how I adore this cocktail – making it and drinking it. It's crisp and fresh and perfectly balanced, when you get it right, and seems delightfully old-fashioned and stylishly modern at the same time.

There is some confusion over its origins. Some say it was created by Harry MacElhone at Harry's New York Bar in Paris, some time around 1919, although he credits it to Pat MacGarry of London's Buck Club. Others say it was the brainchild of the fighter ace pilot, the French-American Raoul Lufbery, or of his squadron, the heroic and glamorous Lafayette Escadrille, during the Great War. Or perhaps it was invented by American officers serving in France, who took it back and popularized it after the war. What is certain, however, is that it is named after the French Howitzer, the French 75mm Field Gun, or Canon de 75 Modèle 1897. These were widely used by the French Artillery and the American Expeditionary Force during the Great War, and in fact a certain Captain Harry S. Truman was in command of a battery of French 75's.

French 75

Ingredients

1½ oz / 4½ cl gin
¾ oz / 2¼ cl freshly squeezed
  lemon juice
½ oz / 1½ cl sugar syrup
Top off with champagne

Preparation

• Shake the first three ingredients
with ice.
• Strain into a chilled flute.
• Carefully top with champagne.
• Garnish with a thin lemon twist.

Tip

Some serve it in a Collins with ice,
but I think it's much cleaner and
nicer in a flute.

Variations

French 76 – **Replace the gin**
with vodka. Try it with cognac,
as some say it was originally
made. You might want to add a
touch more sugar syrup.
French 67 - **I like to crush**
and muddle an inch or two of
cucumber in the base of the
shaker before adding the other
ingredients. Double strain the
contents before topping with
champagne and garnishing with
a spear of cucumber. If you can,
use Hendrick's Gin.

Russian Spring Punch

Russian Spring Punch

Glass
Sling or Collins

While the classic combination may be strawberries and champagne, there's something about raspberries and champagne that just seems to work better for cocktails. There are several combinations of the two ingredients, but I don't think that any beats this one. It's something like a cross between a Daisy and a Collins, but the champagne gives it a transcendent lift. If I may say, with all due respect to its great creator, the unique Dick Bradsell, the name is rather odd.

Ingredients
1 oz / 3 cl vodka
1 oz / 3 cl freshly squeezed lemon juice
½ oz / 1½ cl Crème de Cassis*
¼ oz / ¾ oz sugar syrup
8-10 raspberries
Top off with champagne

Preparation
• Muddle the raspberries in the base of the shaker.
• Add the rest of the ingredients (except champagne) and shake with ice.
• Strain into a glass with ice.**
• Carefully (really!) top off with champagne.
• Garnish with raspberries.***

Tips
* The original recipe calls for Crème de Cassis, and while Cassis may be easier to find, this cocktail surely cries out for the raspberry version, Crème de Framboise, or even Chambord Black Raspberry Liqueur.
** You should use ice cubes, although for some aesthetic reason I much prefer to use crushed ice here.

Recommendations
*** I also like to add a sprig of mint to complement the raspberries.
• How about muddling a small amount of fresh ginger in the shaker before adding the raspberries?

Variations
To make a French Spring Punch, substitute cognac for the vodka. This cocktail would work wonderfully with gin. I mentioned earlier that there are much simpler versions of raspberries and champagne. To make what is either known as

a Metropolis or a Lush , simply mix in a champagne flute:
1 oz / 3 cl chilled vodka
½ oz – 1oz / 1½ cl – 3 cl chilled Crème de Framboise or Chambord
Top off with champagne

Pousse Café & Other Cocktails

06

Pousse
Café
&
Other

Cocktails

Pousse Café, which is an old, old term, literally means push the coffee. It is meant to be something drunk after a meal, as a digestif, in place of coffee. Pousse Cafés are nearly always layered. Careful consideration must also be taken concerning the viscosity, or weight of the ingredients; layers must be built from heavy to light. As a rule, alcohol is lighter than water, having a specific gravity of 1, therefore those ingredients with a higher proof of alcohol are lighter, and go on top.

A Pousse Café can be fun. Here is a list of some of the more popular ones, as well as a few shaken, and not shaken "shots" to keep them company. They should be served in a Pousse Café glass, if you can find one, or a nice shot glass (2 oz / 6 cl minimum), unless otherwise specified. It's often better if the ingredients are chilled ahead of time. Pousse Café is an old term, and there are many, many recipes. You need complete concentration, patience, and a rock steady hand. Here is just one recipe for you. Anymore than that may drive you to drink. Some Pousse Cafés / Shooters invite you to set them alight. Please be careful — remember that flaming liquid spills, dribbles, and can also shatter glass. Be responsible! All ingredients, listed as parts (how much you pour depends on the size of your glass) have to be layered as ordered... Very best of luck!

Americano

Glass

Collins

A fantastic aperitif, not too potent, and as it's topped with soda water, you feel like you're re-hydrating as you drink. The Americano, initially known as the Milano-Torino Cocktail, was invented in the 1860's at Caffe Campari, owned by Gaspare Campari, the inventor of, yes, Campari. Campari hails from Milan, and the other ingredient, Cinzano Rosso (sweet Vermouth) from Turin, hence the name.

The Americano is the first cocktail that we ever see James Bond drinking – right there in Chapter 5 of Casino Royale. While the original is made with Cinzano Rosso, I always use Punt e Mes, which also originates from Turin, so I don't feel bad, as it's still a Milano-Torino. Also, I make mine big. Feel free to reduce the measures, but keep the equal parts ratio.

Ingredients

1½ oz / 4½ cl Campari

1½ oz / 4½ cl sweet vermouth

Top off with soda water

Preparation

• Mix the ingredients in a glass filled with ice.

• Garnish with a large orange slice.

=== **Variations** ===

You can obviously top this up with champagne.

Vermouth

While vermouth is an excellent aperitif by itself, it is also one of the essential ingredients of cocktails. The first commercially produced vermouths of modern times were created by Antonio Carpano of Turin, Italy, but he was not the first to come up with the idea. For a start, the name Vermouth is from the German 'wermut', meaning wormwood (the herb of absinthe infamy) and for a wine spiced with wormwood, among other ingredients. Much further back, the Romans added herbs and spices to their wines, both for medicinal purposes, and to hide the taste of rougher stuff. Vermouth today is usually either dry (white) or sweet (red). There are also sweeter versions such as Martini or Cinzano Bianco, for example. The Sweet is something of a misnomer, for while it has a sweetness to it, it also has bitter notes, which are emphasized in brands such as Punt e Mes. Vermouth is basically fortified wine, infused and flavored with herbs and spices such as cloves, cinnamon, chamomile, juniper, citrus, sage, ginger, coriander seed, star anise, and even rose petals.

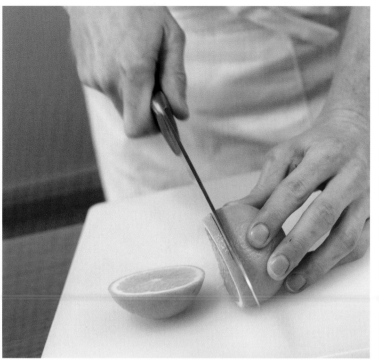

Americano

Grasshopper

Glass
Cocktail

Like many creamy cocktails, and also many luridly colored cocktails – and this is both – the Grasshopper has been stigmatized in recent years. In truth, if you like sweet and creamy cocktails, and let's be honest, we all do once in a blue moon (if no one's looking), this is really rather a cute little number.

The Grasshopper originated in New Orleans, at Tujague's, the second oldest restaurant in the city, and an institution in its own right. In 1914, Guillame Tujague sold his interest to Philibert Guichet from Guichetville, Raceland. Five years later, 1919, Guichet would come second place in the prestigious New York Cocktail Competition with his Grasshopper, which has been famous ever since (despite Prohibition starting in the same year).

=== Variations ===
Flying Grasshopper – **replace the cream with 1 oz / 3 cl vodka.**

Grasshopper

Ingredients

1 oz / 3 cl green Crème de Menthe
1 oz / 3 cl white Crème de Cacao
1½ oz / 4½ cl heavy cream

Preparation

• Shake all the ingredients
vigorously with ice.
• Double strain into a chilled glass.

Tip

It's important to use the green
and white Crèmes, both for the
taste and the color. Brown Crème
de Cacao would give a different
taste, and a fairly unappealing
color. Add more or less cream
as you wish.

Liqueurs

The subject of liqueurs is rather confusing. Essentially, a liqueur is
an alcoholic beverage that has been flavored and sweetened with
sugars, those flavorings including fruits (and I mean the term in its
very broadest sense, to include, somewhat erroneously, I know,
coffee, cacao, nuts etc), plants, herbs, spices, cream and so on. While
a melon-flavored vodka will be vodka with melon flavoring and no
added sugar (or at least a restricted amount), a melon liqueur can
be based on any spirit, and will be sweetened. In America, schnapps
also tend to be liqueurs, while in Europe the name is synonymous
with the fruit-based Eaux-de-Vies, predominantly found in Germany.
We should also clarify the term Crème, as in Crème de Cassis, or
Crème de Menthe, which actually contain no cream whatsoever,
but are thickened (usually with sugar) until they have a cream-like
consistency. Not, of course, to be confused with Cream Liqueurs, such
as Irish Cream, which does contain cream (and coffee and whisky).

Sangria
(& Mulled Wine)

Glass
Pitcher

If you're making Sangria for yourself, then I guess you should go ahead and make it however you like, but if you're entertaining, then my advice would be less is more; keep it simple. If you use a decent bottle of wine, it will do most of the work for you. Build it slowly, tasting and testing all the time – let your recipe evolve over time, see what you and other people like and don't like. While I personally love spices, I would tend to avoid using them in Sangria, because they are so divisive. Furthermore, spices are hard to use in a cold drink (they don't mix so well, or impart so much flavor), unless you infuse them in the wine before hand. Use the following as a foundation for your Sangria, on which you can test additional ingredients. And remember – it's wine, not Grape Liqueur: GO EASY ON THE SWEET STUFF.

Ingredients

1 bottle of red wine* (75cl)
4 oz / 12 cl Grand Marnier
   (if not, Cointreau)
2 oz / 6 cl cognac (optional)**
1 cup freshly squeezed orange
   juice
1 oz / 3 cl freshly squeezed lemon
   juice
1 oz – 2oz / 3 cl – 6cl sugar
   syrup***
Chunks of seasonable fruit****
3 dashes of Angostura Bitters

Preparation

• Serve chilled with lots of ice.

Tips

* Use a fruity, young wine – not too heavy or oaky. A young Rioja is ideal – just don't be cheap!
** Some do some don't. I also recommend a good aged rum, but not dark.
*** The amount of sugar will depend on your wine, the lemons and the oranges, so start with 1 oz / 3 cl, taste and add in moderation. Honey can also be nice. Or even vanilla syrup.
**** I love having a lot of fruit in my drinks – you could serve it with a spoon. Just don't use something with too strong a taste or too much juice that will change the flavor, like passion fruit. Berries, melon, apples, and citrus fruits are ideal.

• Ginger anyone? You can always top off your Sangria with soda water, although I'm not a fan. Just don't – please don't! – use Sprite or 7-Up or something similar.

Bitters

A curious and slightly misleading catchall category, that encompasses such marvels as Angostura Bitters, Campari and Fernet Branca, to name but three. Most bitters were created for medicinal purposes, especially as aids to digestion. They are the highly aromatic, herbal, spicy concoctions that are usually drunk as a digestif, but can, as with Campari, be taken as an aperitif. Bitters often include such ingredients as quinine, the bark of the angostura trifoliata plant, and the curative gentian, amongst many others. Cocktail bitters are extremely concentrated in flavor. They are rather like condiments, and you will often hear them referred to as cocktail seasoning – just a dash or two is required to add an extra dynamic to a drink.

Variations

Sangria Blanca

You can also make a white wine version. Use something dry, light and crisp – not a buttery, oaky Chardonnay.

I'd leave out the orange juice, although a splash or two of freshly pressed pineapple juice could be nice. If you have access to elderflower liqueur, I strongly recommend adding some. I would leave out the cognac or rum. I sometimes, not always, add some Crème de Cassis, or Framboise, just to be mischievous.

Sangria

B-52

Glass
Pousse Café or Shot

Pousse Café is an old term, and there are many, many recipes. You need complete concentration, patience, and a rock steady hand. Here is just one recipe for you. Anymore than that may drive you to drink. Some Pousse Cafés / Shooters invite you to set them alight. Please be careful – remember that flaming liquid spills, dribbles, and can also shatter glass. Be responsible!

Definitely one of the best known and most popular Pousse Cafés. Believed to be named after the B-52 bombers that were used to such devastating effect in the Vietnam War.

Ingredients
½ oz / 1½ cl Kahlua
½ oz / 1½ cl Bailey's Irish Cream
  (or other brand)
½ oz / 1½ cl Grand Marnier

Preparation
• Carefully layer the ingredients as above.

Tip
Although not as suitable or effective, Cointreau can be used in place of Grand Marnier.

══════ **Variations** ══════
There are several variations on the B-52, mainly involving the last ingredient. The most popular liqueurs with which to replace the Grand Marnier are vodka, tequila, absinthe, Galliano or Green Chartreuse. I'll leave you to figure out which ones are worth trying.

B-52

Purple Haze

Glass
Pousse Café or Shot

A cute little drink that I think I must have made thousands of... A great one for entertaining.

Purple Haze

Ingredients

1½ oz / 4½ cl vodka

½ oz / 1½ cl freshly squeezed
   lime juice

¼ oz / ¾ cl sugar syrup

Dash of Chambord liqueur

Preparation

• Shake the first three ingredients
with ice.

• Strain into a chilled glass.

• Gently pour the Chambord
down the side of the glass to
create the haze.

Sangrita

Glass
Pousse Café or Shot

A shot of Sangrita is actually only part of either a Completo or a Bandera, both of which are traditional Mexican Tequila orders. The Sangrita, meaning 'little blood,' is a shot of spicy juice, designed to compliment the sour, spicy taste of a simple tequila. When you order a Completo you receive a shot of tequila and a separate shot of Sangrita. In a Bandera, you also receive a third shot of fresh lime juice, which together with the Tequila and Sangrita represent the Mexican Flag (green – lime, white – tequila, and red – Sangrita).

There are several versions of Sangrita – Mexican and other. The other version uses tomato juice in the recipe, along with orange and / or grenadine. The Mexican, or to be more precise, the Jalisco (the state where Tequila is produced) version is a soured combination of orange and pomegranate juices. Both versions sometimes use onion. Obviously, pomegranates are pretty hard to come by so you'll have to use a grenadine syrup – but try to find one based on actual pomegranate.

There are no set rules for making Sangrita but the following are fairly common versions:
Completo – shot of tequila and shot of Sangrita
Bandera – shot of tequila, shot of Sangrita, and shot of fresh lime juice

Sangrita Recipe – Jalisco style

Ingredients
Either
1 oz / 3 cl freshly squeezed orange juice (the sourer, the better)
1 oz / 3 cl freshly pressed pomegranate juice
Or
¼ oz / ¾ cl grenadine (you can use more if it's not too sweet)
½ oz / 1½ cl freshly squeezed lime juice (adjust to the sourness of your oranges)
Hot Sauce / chili powder / minced fresh Serrano or Jalapeño chili to taste
2 bar spoons of finely chopped or minced onion – optional
Salt to taste – optional

Sangrita Recipe – Gringo style

Ingredients
1 oz / 3 cl tomato juice
½ oz / 1½ cl freshly squeezed orange juice
½ oz / 1½ cl freshly squeezed lime juice
1 teaspoon grenadine (optional)
Hot Sauce / chili powder / minced fresh Serrano or Jalapeños chili to taste
2 bar spoons of finely chopped or minced onion – optional
Salt and pepper to taste – optional

Preparation
• For best results, make these recipes up ahead of time and refrigerate, and strain before using. The flavors will marinade and you don't have to dilute them with ice, or change the texture by blending.

Sangrita

Acknowledgments

I cannot possibly express how much I have been influenced by the work of many people. First of all, I believe in keeping an open mind, and I don't think there has ever been a bartender I worked with that I didn't learn from – even if it was how not to do something. Among the many names and faces of which so many are a blur, I would like to thank my good friends, David Miles, Nala, Richard Elvis, Barrett Young, Ilan Avitsur, Anya for her timely criticism and a whole lot more, and two great teachers, Dick Bradsell and Wayne Collins, and all the team from Odeon, for some of the very best of times, memories, and lessons in both bartending and life. But most of all, I owe all of this to my family, Yael, Romi, Mia and Alma, for putting up with me and my ridiculous hours, for their patience and support (both generally, but especially during the writing of this book!), and most of all for making me realize that, however much I love my job, there's so very much more to life than standing behind, or sitting at, a bar.

Index